The Silver Man

THE SILVER MAN

The Life and Times of Indian Agent John Kinzie

PETER SHRAKE

WISCONSIN HISTORICAL SOCIETY PRESS

Published by the Wisconsin Historical Society Press
Publishers since 1855

© 2016 by the State Historical Society of Wisconsin

wisconsinhistory.org

Photographs identified with WHi or WHS are from the Society's collections; address requests to reproduce these photos to the Visual Materials Archivist at the Wisconsin Historical Society, 816 State Street, Madison, WI 53706.

Printed in Wisconsin, USA
Designed by Ryan Scheife / Mayfly Design

20 19 18 17 16   1 2 3 4 5

Library of Congress Cataloging-in-Publication Data
Shrake, Peter.
  The silver man : the life and times of Indian Agent John Kinzie / Peter Shrake. — 1st edition.
     pages cm
  Includes bibliographical references and index.
  ISBN 978-0-87020-740-2 (pbk.) — ISBN 978-0-87020-741-9 (e-book) 1. Kinzie, John H., 1803–1865. 2. Ho Chunk Indians—Government relations—History—19th century. 3. Indian agents—United States—Biography 4. Ho Chunk Indians—Wars. 5. Fort Winnebago (Wis.)—History. 6. Frontier and pioneer life—Wisconsin. 7. Wisconsin—History—19th century. 8. Wisconsin—Biography. I. Title.
  E99.W7S54 2016
  323.1197'526—dc23
                          2015034624

For Dad

Publication of this book was made possible in part through a generous grant from The National Society of The Colonial Dames of America in the State of Wisconsin.

The Indian Agency House, built for John Kinzie and now owned and operated by The National Society of The Colonial Dames in the State of Wisconsin. COURTESY OF DELLA NOHL

Contents

Acknowledgments

I have learned many things while writing this book, but chief among them is the realization that a book is not just the efforts of one individual. It is, in reality, a group project. Certainly there is an author, but that author is supported and assisted by a broad range of individuals who all in some way made critical contributions to the project.

This book first started with an invitation by Destinee Udelhoven, the former Director of the Historic Indian Agency House to deliver a presentation on the career of John H. Kinzie in 2010. That lecture in turn led to an article published in the Wisconsin Magazine of History two years later. It was the Board of Directors of the Wisconsin Chapter of The National Society of The Colonial Dames of America (the organization that owns and administers the Historic Indian Agency House), most notably Anne Vravic, who first raised the idea of expanding the article into a book. I was not sure I wanted to tackle such a project, but Anne was persistent. Her constant encouragement ultimately culminated in the work you see here. It also must be acknowledged that the board generously provided funding to help with research and publishing.

The Colonial Dames were the spark, but the editorial staff at the Wisconsin Historical Society Press carried the heavy load of transforming a mass of words into a cohesive manuscript. Director Kathy Borkowski provided endless encouragement. Senior Editor Kate Thompson exhibited great patience waiting for a first draft as I blew past several deadlines. My greatest debt is to Developmental Editor Carrie Kilman, who worked with me to forge the manuscript into its final form.

As an archivist it would be impossible for me not to acknowledge the kind assistance of staff at the Museum of the Confederacy, Chicago Historical Museum, Newberry Library, Kenyon College, and the Wisconsin Historical Society. Though I imagine many would say they were merely doing their job, it is by doing their job that people like me can do projects such as this.

Finally, this book would not have been possible were it not for the patience and support of my family. There were many days when my mom,

Kathy Shrake, watched the kids and provided me many quiet hours to write. My wife, Kim, not only watched the kids but also had to endure countless impromptu lectures about Jacksonian Indian Policy and John Kinzie, as well as live with a husband who forever has his head stuck in the far distant past. But it was my two boys, Ben and Ethan, who really made the greatest effort. For over a year, both boys, both under the age of ten, displayed incredible understanding and patience (they actually hate that word despite my best efforts) as their dad worked from behind closed doors.

A book project is indeed the culmination of the efforts of many, but in the end the final responsibility for its accuracy lies with the author. Any and all errors or omissions found within are mine and mine alone.

—PETER SHRAKE

INTRODUCTION

In the early nineteenth century, the portage between the Fox and Wisconsin Rivers was an isolated place. Located deep in the Wisconsin interior, the area had a marshy quality, with open rolling hills edged by oak groves.[1] Only a mile and a half separated the two rivers. This narrow strip of land helped to connect the Great Lakes with the Mississippi River. From Lake Michigan, travelers heading west could take the Fox River to the portage, cross over land to the Wisconsin River, and follow it to the Mississippi—with the course reversed for travelers heading east. As a result, the Fox–Wisconsin waterway quickly became an important northern highway.

Several local businesses provided aid to travelers as they made the crossing between the two rivers, and the American Fur Company maintained a post there. The portage was also where the territory for the Ojibwe, Menominee, and Ho-Chunk tribes converged.

For all of the portage's strategic and economic importance, the federal government never intended to establish an Indian agency or a military installation there. Indian affairs were guided by agencies at Green Bay, Fort Snelling, Prairie du Chien, and Chicago. But a series of events, beginning with the end of the War of 1812 and culminating in a crisis in the summer of 1827, changed the opinion of officials in Washington, and in 1828 Fort Winnebago and its accompanying Indian subagency would be established approximately 1.5 miles northeast of the Wisconsin River on a hilltop overlooking the Fox River.

In the years following the War of 1812, Wisconsin was a region grappling with transitions. One empire, Great Britain, was receding, and a new one, the United States, was on the rise. Population dynamics were in flux as Yankees from New England and southerners from Missouri, Kentucky, Tennessee, and the Carolinas were pushing against the various Native tribes and the old French and mixed-ancestry inhabitants. The economy was shifting, from the fur trade to mining, lumber, milling, and agriculture. The two main communities in the region were still Prairie du Chien and Green Bay, but with the advent of lead mining, countless new settlements were springing up south of the Wisconsin River. Despite

all of this change, the Michigan Territory, which included present-day
Wisconsin, was still a remote territory. The principal seat of government
lay hundreds of miles away in Detroit, the capital of Michigan Territory.
Law was the domain of the US Army, local justices of the peace, and later
James Duane Doty, who presided over the Additional Court of the territory
in Green Bay.[2]

Throughout the War of 1812, the western Great Lakes region was controlled by the British. The Treaty of Ghent, which ended the war on December 24, 1814, stipulated that British forces withdraw from the area.
It would be two years, however, before the Americans would be able to
physically take control of Wisconsin.

In 1816, contingents of the US Army landed, almost simultaneously,
at both Green Bay and Prairie du Chien. The inhabitants of the region—
white, mixed ancestry (or people of both French and Indian lineage), and
Indian—were uneasy at the arrival of the Americans and were unsure how
the new rulers would treat them.[3]

For each group, the American arrival would mean different fates. For
the British who didn't flee, it was possible to slowly incorporate themselves
into the new order of things. For the inhabitants of mixed ancestry, times
would be harsh for a while; like many of the tribes living around them, they
had fought in and often led many of the campaigns against the Americans
in the recent war. As a result, the Americans would exclude them from
the fur trade, the very source of their income and livelihood. This policy
resulted in a long relationship of animosity between the mixed-ancestry
population and the federal government. For the Indians, the arrival of
the US Army would mean a more difficult relationship with a new nation.

Our story takes places in this period of transition.

John H. Kinzie came to adulthood in the years immediately following
the War of 1812. His tenure as Indian agent at the portage chronicles a period of significant change for the Ho-Chunk—or the Winnebago, as they
were called by most white settlers, fur traders, and government officials
during the nineteenth century—as they struggled come to terms with
American advancement into the Upper Midwest.

Much of what we know about John Kinzie comes from the writings
of his wife, Juliette Magill Kinzie. Juliette's best-known work, a memoir
titled *Wau-Bun: The "Early Day" in the North-West,* describes the three

years she and John lived at the portage. First published in 1856, *Wau-Bun* remains an often-quoted resource on life and Indian–white relations in early-nineteenth-century Wisconsin.

Fifteen years after writing *Wau-Bun*, Juliette wrote a supplemental biographical sketch of John for the Chicago Historical Society. These two works of writing give us the image of a man who was affable, unassuming, well liked, and good at his job. But in some respects, Juliette's account of the life of an Indian agent is superficial. Very little is mentioned of John Kinzie's first year as subagent, and from her writing it would appear that the main reason for Kinzie's presence in Wisconsin was to make annuity payments and take long trips around the region. This is not a criticism, rather more of a reflection on the realities of marriage. How many people can really describe, in detail, the professional lives of their spouse? *Wau-Bun* is first and foremost Juliette's story. John Kinzie is an important but secondary character.

Exploring John Kinzie's story not only provides context to Juliette's writings, it also gives us the opportunity to examine the role of the Indian agent, a lower-level but important bureaucrat who administered, interpreted, and guided Indian affairs along the western frontier of the United States in the early and often tumultuous years of the expanding Union. Indian agents held significant power. They controlled when and where annuity payments were made to Native communities, and they controlled tribal access to the federal government. If a tribal leader wanted to convey messages to the territorial governor or the president, they had to go through their local Indian agent. Indian policy was set by politicians and bureaucrats in Washington or worked out in numerous treaty negotiations. Agents represented that policy and functioned as a daily point of contact between two cultures. If we wish to understand life on the Wisconsin frontier and the relationship between Native American and white communities—a relationship that is still playing out today—then we must understand the Indian agent.

We encounter two challenges when trying to learn about Kinzie's life. First, none of his personal papers are known to exist. In a paper read before the Chicago Historical Society in 1868, Juliette referred to a journal John kept, but that resource, along with so many family papers, was most likely destroyed in the Chicago fire of 1871. This is unfortunate—for the second challenge is that Kinzie witnessed so many of the great events of his day. He was present at the Fort Dearborn massacre. He came of age working in the fur trade. He attended a number of important treaty councils, witnessed the shooting of Alexis St. Martin, experienced the Black Hawk War, and knew personally many of the notable personalities of the region, including Lewis Cass, Robert Stuart, Ramsay Crooks, and Pierre Paquette. He knew or had knowledge of many of the great Indian leaders, including Four Legs, White Crow, and Nawkaw Caramaunee, and was a student of their culture and language. He experienced all of this before relocating permanently to Chicago and taking a firsthand role in the development of that great city. Constructing a biography that includes these events and characters with limited primary source material is difficult at best.

Luckily, some of Kinzie's professional correspondence as Indian sub-agent does exist. Likewise, we get glimpses of him in various letters or documents written by others. But the only way to understand his life is to explore in detail the events he experienced. A biography of John Harris Kinzie must be a history of the times in which he lived.

This book is not a social history of Wisconsin during the early nineteenth century. A number of excellent books already fill that role. Neither is this an in-depth history of the Ho-Chunk Nation—though the tribe is an integral part of John Kinzie's story, and consequently this book chronicles a crucial period in which the Ho-Chunk people grappled with radical change. This book is merely an attempt to document the life of a man, and in that attempt provide a broader view of the world in which he lived, a world that in no small part forms a foundation for the world in which we live today.

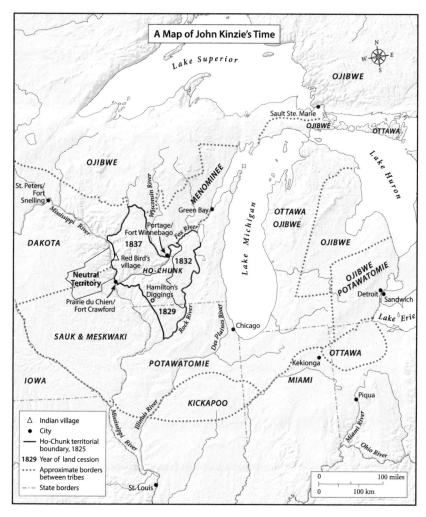

A Map of John Kinzie's Time

Kinzie and his family witnessed many rapid changes across the Midwestern frontier throughout the early and mid-1800s. MAPPING SPECIALISTS, LTD., FITCHBURG, WI

1

On the Road

Juliette Kinzie looked out from her makeshift tent and was alarmed by what she saw. "Around us was an unbroken sheet of snow," she would write in *Wau-Bun*.

> We had no compass, and the air was so obscured by the driving sleet, that it was often impossible to tell in which direction the sun was. I tied my husband's silk pocket handkerchief over my veil, to protect my face from the wind and icy particles with which the air was filled, and which cut like a razor; but although shielded in every way that circumstances rendered possible, I suffered intensely from the cold.[1]

Juliette's husband, John Harris Kinzie, had taken temporary leave of his duties as Indian subagent at Fort Winnebago and was traveling with his wife to Chicago. He had important family business to attend to, and he had already put off the trip for several months. The original plan had been to travel in January, but a heavy snowfall delayed them when the post commandant, Major David Twiggs, threatened to order the fort sentinels to fire on anyone leaving the fort.[2]

Now it was the middle of March 1831. The plan was to travel due south for Dixon's Ferry, cross the Rock River, and strike east for Lake Michigan. The weather had been cooperative at the start, but a day or so after passing the Four Lakes—present-day Madison, Wisconsin—the weather turned. They were traveling through unfamiliar country. Though he had been raised in Chicago and the Great Lakes region, John Kinzie was more

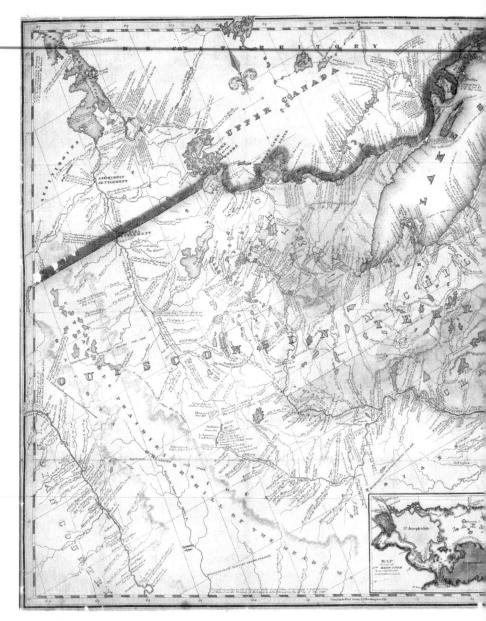

A map of the Michigan Territory, 1831. This map was used by officers at Fort Winnebago and possibly John Kinzie. WHI IMAGE ID 41281

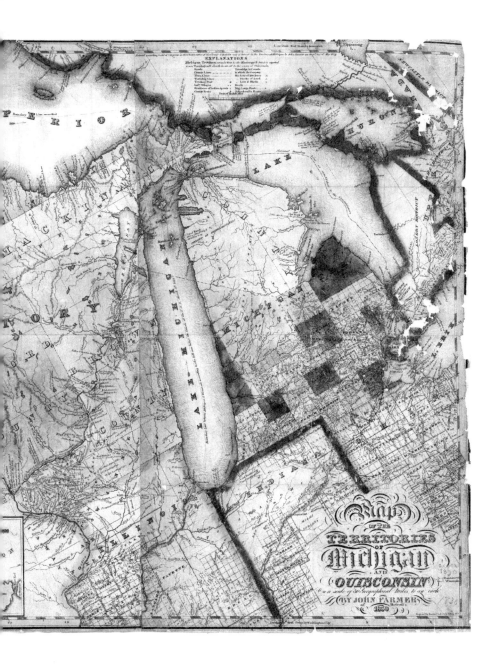

familiar with the trails to the east, closer to Lake Michigan, and their guide, as they discovered, was unreliable.

They were lost. As the group plodded onward, each stand of woods brought hope of running into a settlement or an Indian encampment, where someone could tell them where they were. After traveling for several miles, someone spotted a fence line. Excitement among the group was palpable; they followed the fence until they came to a small cluster of cabins. John saw a man cutting wood and called out, "Whose cabins are those?"

"Hamilton's," the man hollered back.

Soon the traveling party was indoors, warming by the fire. Juliette was overjoyed, but she noted with guarded curiosity the men who surrounded them.

> They were the roughest-looking set of men I ever beheld, and their language was as uncouth as their persons. They wore hunting-shirts, trowsers, and moccasins of deerskin, the former being ornamented at the seams with a fringe of the same, while a colored belt around the waist, in which was stuck a large hunting-knife, gave each the appearance of a brigand. [3]

They were lead miners, men seeking fortune in the grey gold that dotted the southwestern Wisconsin countryside.

John most likely shared Juliette's mixed feelings. Though certainly he must have been relieved to be out of the storm, the situation had put him in the company of William S. Hamilton, son of founding father Alexander Hamilton. Only three months earlier, William Hamilton had sent John a bristling letter complaining about the ineptitude of the Indian department and of Kinzie in particular. Hamilton claimed that earlier that fall, several Ho-Chunk had broken into the cabin of one of his miners and robbed it. Many of the items taken from the cabin were later found in the possession of Woank-shik-rootsh-kay, or Man Eater, a prominent leader of the Rock River Band of Ho-Chunk.

That fall, when the Ho-Chunk people gathered to receive their annual annuity payment, Hamilton and others in his community had sought reimbursement for their losses. Kinzie denied their demands, later reporting, "Several claims were acknowledged and paid by the Indians, and I was requested by them in council *not to pay any claim* against them, as they believed the white people wanted to cheat them out of all their money."[4]

The situation was serious enough that Kinzie felt he had to write to the Secretary of War to defend his actions. He pointed out that he was following direct instructions from his superior, Michigan Territorial Governor Lewis Cass. "All these dissensions, between the Indians and the miners, are on the borders of the Indian line, where are scattered 8 to 10 huts, inhabited by persons, many of whom are regardless of honesty and ready for any adventure."[5] The same chief, Man Eater, lodged a similar complaint, claiming to Kinzie that he had been robbed of two guns by a man from Hamilton's group.

Hamilton, for his part, was equally disgusted and wrote to Kinzie:

The *little faith* I have in the *Indian Department* has compelled me to adopt a system of retaliation, and I have determined in all instances to pursue the aggressors, retake the property, and allow the persons in company with me to take property enough from the Indians to pay them for their trouble and in some instances to [use] the lash, *your interference* will only make the thing worse.[6]

Hamilton went on to complain, "If proper [exertion] was used by the Indian department, these evil might be avoided but on the [contrary] rumor say that the course pursued by you at the portage has had a tendency to increase instead of diminishing the [sort] if *true* as told me, you may [expect] to hear from Washington."[7]

Kinzie thought he knew where the real problem lay. The annuity payments were made at the Indian subagency, next door to Fort Winnebago, and not somewhere amid the miners or fur traders where "they could have a good opportunity of selling to those Indians, liquor in any quantity."[8]

Kinzie had merely been doing his job. As the subagent at Fort Winnebago, Kinzie distributed the annual annuity payments owed to the Ho-Chunk as a result of past treaty agreements. At the time of each payment, Kinzie was besieged by creditors, local miners, fur traders, and other businessmen who all claimed debts owed to them by the tribe. Kinzie had to determine which claims were fair and which were not. When Kinzie asked them to submit their claims in proper form with evidence, the

miners refused, leading Kinzie to doubt
their authenticity.

"I feel confident that more depredations are complained of, than
are actually committed," Kinzie
wrote. In addition, the claimants
often filed for reimbursement
far beyond the value of the actual
property damaged or stolen.[9]

The altercation with Hamilton underscored the complexi-
ties of the life of an Indian agent
and stemmed from the imperfect
system of federal regulations regarding Indian affairs. As one of
the few federal officials on the
frontier, the Indian agent had
the unenviable job of protecting
government interests while at the

William S. Hamilton, son of Alexander Hamilton and owner of a lead mining operation
in southwestern Wisconsin. WHI IMAGE ID 3458

same time looking out for the welfare of the Native Americans living in
their jurisdiction—all while dealing with private citizens chafing at a set of
vague federal laws. Indian agents such as Kinzie often found themselves at
odds with either local settlers, other Indian agents, or the powerful American Fur Company.

Since the founding of the republic, the formal relationship between
the United States and the different Indian tribes was the responsibility
of the executive branch and fell under the supervision of the Secretary of
War. Federal Indian policy, however, was not well defined. Between 1790
and 1800, Congress enacted seventeen laws providing new regulations or
revising existing ones for federal officials to follow. These laws were aug-
mented by treaties with individual tribes, which effectively meant policy
could vary from tribe to tribe or region to region.[10]

· In 1802, Congress enacted a new Trade and Intercourse Act intended to
iron out the inconsistencies of previous laws and provide a universal set of
rules governing all Indian affairs along the frontier. Even though Congress
would enact another twenty-eight new laws before Kinzie received his

appointment as Indian subagent in 1828, the Trade and Intercourse Act of 1802 would stand as the principal law guiding the actions of Indian agents and regulated the relationship between the two cultures for twenty-two years. The act also placed the US Army in the difficult role of frontier police, serving as a physical barrier between settlers and Indians and intervening whenever crimes such as murders were committed, whether the culprits were Indian or white.

Indian affairs were supervised regionally by superintendents of Indian affairs. Superintendents were intended to be independent offices, but as a cost-saving measure the task was often assigned directly to local territorial governors, leading to not only overworked officials but also a serious conflict of interest. Superintendents were charged with looking after the welfare of the tribes and enforcing federal law, duties that often were at odds with the actions and desires of the civil population that these same men served as territorial governors. Indian affairs in Wisconsin were directed by two superintendents, with the portage sitting at roughly the halfway point between them. Lewis Cass, the territorial governor of Michigan, covered the eastern Great Lakes region; William Clark oversaw matters on the Mississippi River Valley and westward from his office in St. Louis.[11]

Daily interactions were handled by Indian agents who were assigned regionally to specific tribes. Subagents were assistants to the full agents; however, it was not unusual for a subagent to act independently and with the authority of a full agent—as Kinzie did—if a full agent wasn't stationed nearby. In these circumstances, a subagent had all of the responsibilities of a full agent but without the benefit of additional pay.

Indian tribes are and were sovereign entities; as a result, an Indian agent was something like a diplomat residing in a foreign nation. The agent served as the principal point of regular communications between the federal government and the different tribes. As new policies and treaty terms were established, the agent explained these matters to the leaders of the tribe. Similarly, if the tribe had any important matters or problems, they could bring them before their local agent. Indian agents were observers, carefully watching and listening to the various activities in their regions. They were a weather gauge for how a particular tribe might respond to a crisis or a treaty proposal.

—◄||►—

As the snowstorm raged, the Kinzies and their fellow travelers spent the better part of the day cooped up in Hamilton's cabin. If Kinzie and Hamilton exchanged words during that March afternoon, they went unrecorded. Juliette had nothing but kind words for their host but did note shortly after they arrived at Hamilton's that her husband was "a long time absent." Perhaps the two men worked out their disagreements before entering the cabin.

Regardless of the matter, once the storm had cleared, Hamilton led the party to his nearest neighbor, and the Kinzies were on their way. Their journey was long and difficult. The weather continued to be uncooperative. After safely crossing the Rock River at Dixon's Ferry, the group again lost direction and ran low on supplies. At long last the party ran into a small Potawatomi village, and soon familiar landmarks came into view—they had arrived at Chicago.

Chicago was still a small trading village in 1831. It centered around Fort Dearborn, which sat on the south side of the Chicago River where it emptied into Lake Michigan. Just across the river on the north bank stood the Kinzie homestead. The previous September the family had been notified by the federal government that they were entitled to claim lands around the family home. During that spring visit, John and his brother Robert spent several weeks surveying the family claim and preparing the necessary paperwork.[12]

In a few weeks the job was done, and in April Kinzie returned to Fort Winnebago alone, leaving Juliette with his family. Two months later he was back at Chicago, this time to bring Juliette and his mother, his sister, and her son back to the portage to live at the agency.

The spring of 1831 was foretelling of Kinzie's career in the Indian field service. Long journeys and personal business constantly took him away from his duties. Chicago would continuously call to him. It was where he spent much of his childhood, but now, as a result of his spring travels, it would also be his future. The land claim he plotted out with his brother would eventually bring the family a fortune.

2

YOUNG JOHN KINZIE

It was by accident that John Harris Kinzie was not born in the United States. His mother, Eleanor Lytle Kinzie, was visiting her sister in Sandwich, Ontario, when, on July 7, 1803, she gave birth to a healthy baby boy. Named after his father, John Harris Kinzie would grow up in a household that saw occasional success, frequent failure, the brutality of battle, and the uncertainty of life along the frontier.

John Kinzie Sr. was fifty years old when his namesake was born. He was a well-established fur trader on the western Great Lakes, operating in the Chicago, Milwaukee, and Illinois country at a time when John J. Astor of the American Fur Company was just starting to spread his operations into the Great Lakes region. The son of a British army surgeon, the older Kinzie originally began his working life as a silversmith in Montreal. The job had little appeal to the Quebec native, but the silver brooches, crosses, armbands, and other trinkets he made and used for barter in the fur trade provided a glimpse into another career and allowed him to develop important business contacts. It was not long before he made the switch from silversmith to fur trader.[1]

During the 1780s, while operating at Kekionga near what is today Fort Wayne, Indiana, Kinzie developed a relationship with Margaret McKenzie, a Virginia native and Shawnee captive who eventually bore him three children. As children, Margaret and a sister had been taken captive when the Shawnee attacked their Virginia homestead, killing their mother and other siblings. Their father had been away on business when his family was attacked, but he never forgot the children who had been taken away. After nearly twenty years, Margaret's father found his daughters, and Marga-

ret left Kinzie and returned to
Virginia with their children.

A few years later, in 1798,
Kinzie met and married Eleanor Lytle, who herself had
been previously married and
had a child. Born in 1769, Eleanor had spent several years
as a captive of the Seneca
Indians. Kinzie and Eleanor
would eventually have five
children in all; John Harris
was the couple's second child;
their first had died in infancy.
John Harris was followed by
sisters Ellen Marion in 1804

A silver cross made by John Kinzie Sr. CHICAGO
HISTORY MUSEUM, ICHI 64676; KINZIE, JOHN, CREATOR

and Maria Indiana in 1807, and brother Robert Allen in 1810.[2]

Throughout his early life, John Kinzie Sr. had allied himself with British interests and pro-British traders. But after the Revolutionary War, he
became an American citizen. The Jay Treaty of 1794 required that residents
living in the United States declare their British nationality or automatically
become US citizens. As a result, Kinzie was an American citizen more by
default than by choice.

It was a precarious way of life. Shifting political realities and wars
along the Ohio River Valley could wreak havoc on those working in the
fur trade. In 1791, the home Kinzie shared with his first family at Kekionga
was burned by American forces operating against the Miami. They moved
thirty-five miles north to the small settlement of Au Glaize. Three years
later their homestead was again destroyed—this time as a result of the
campaigns of 1794 and the Battle of Fallen Timbers.[3]

By 1803 John Kinzie Sr. had settled his family in Chicago. While he
continued his involvement in the fur trade, he also developed other businesses, such as providing supplies to Fort Dearborn. Business was good,
and in the years leading up to the War of 1812 the Kinzie home had become
the largest in Chicago. The family owned four slaves, including a married
couple, Athena and Henry. Athena performed household chores and was

This illustration, ca. 1820, shows Fort Dearborn, center, and the Kinzie mansion, far right. WHI IMAGE ID 28328

the family cook, while Henry and two other slaves, Black Jim and Pepper, worked the garden beds and assisted Kinzie with his trading business.[4] The Kinzie family also employed a number of individuals of mixed ancestry. All in all, perhaps as many as seventeen people lived and worked at the Kinzie place. It was a busy household and an often-used rest stop for travelers as they prepared to make the portage between the Des Plaines River and Lake Michigan.[5]

Described by some as a domineering man with a quick temper, Kinzie was a controversial figure. He was suspected of being a spy by both Americans and British before the War of 1812. He was also a known murderer who killed his neighbor and business rival Jean B. La Lime in a fight in the spring of 1812. The two men had been at odds for some time and on previous occasions had had serious arguments. La Lime was an independent fur trader and interpreter for federal officials in the area. The specific reasons for their final fight are not clear, but it was most likely business related. The two men met outside the walls of Fort Dearborn, La Lime with a pistol and Kinzie with a butcher's knife. When the fight was over, La Lime was dead and Kinzie wounded. After La Lime's death, Kinzie fled Chicago, eventually hiding out near Milwaukee, where he had established good relations with the local Potawatomi. While at Milwaukee he attended a council of Potawatomi leaders and learned of their impending attack on Fort Dearborn.[6]

No formal investigation into the murder was ever conducted, and many people, especially within the Kinzie family, maintained that Kinzie killed La Lime in self-defense. Kinzie returned to Chicago in August and passed on his knowledge of the impending attack to Captain Heald, the commandant of Fort Dearborn.

On August 9, 1812, Heald received a letter from General William Hull at Detroit ordering him to evacuate Fort Dearborn.[7] War had broken out between the United States and Great Britain that June, and British forces had already seized Mackinac Island. The pro-British stance of the Potawatomi was well known, and Chicago was an isolated outpost with a garrison of only sixty-nine men. Six days after receiving Hull's letter, Heald led his garrison, the local militia, and the soldiers' families, along with a small group of friendly Miami Indians, out of Fort Dearborn. A little over a mile from the fort, amid the sand dunes along the Lake Michigan shoreline, the group was attacked. The militia and their families were killed. Heald was seriously wounded and captured, along with about twenty-eight regular soldiers.

Though John Kinzie Sr. was with the garrison, he had had the forethought to place his entire household, including his family, slaves, and clerks, as well as significant personal belongings, onto a bateaux—a shallow, flat-bottomed boat common then in the western Great Lakes—that remained anchored offshore near the mouth of the Chicago River.[8] The family did not witness the carnage as the Potawatomi attacked, driving the American soldiers into the dunes against the lakeshore. Nor did they see the slaughter of the garrison families, but they could hear it. From their bateaux, as Eleanor Kinzie remembered, "They had seen the smoke—then the blaze—and immediately after, the report of the first tremendous discharge sounded in their ears. Then all was confusion."[9]

The Kinzie family was spared during the battle, possibly on the order the Potawatomi chief Black Partridge, and afterward the family was under the chief's protection. Using what influence and trade goods he had left, Kinzie negotiated the release of Captain Heald.[10] Chicago was not safe after the massacre of the American garrison; as soon as the Potawatomi left the settlement, Kinzie fled with his family to Detroit, remaining there for four years.

The family's economic condition at this time must have been precarious. This was the third time Kinzie saw his business destroyed and his family uprooted. But this time, his duplicitous behavior caught up with him; about a year after fleeing to Detroit, he was arrested by the British, who believed Kinzie was encouraging the Potawatomi to make a separate peace with the United States.

Little is recorded about John Harris Kinzie Jr. during these years. There is no evidence to suggest that his childhood before the War of 1812 was unhappy. His education before the age of nine took place at the family's Chicago's home. Chicago was an isolated place during those years, and access to the settlement was either overland through the wilderness or by passage on a schooner, which visited the settlement once a year. When the schooner visited Chicago in 1809, the year John Kinzie was six years old, a spelling book was discovered in a chest of green tea. John's thirteen-year-old cousin, Robert Allen Forsyth, took it upon himself to teach the young boy the alphabet, but John was a stubborn student, and soon the project was abandoned.[11] But the memory of the experience lingered—even when John was an adult, green tea would bring back memories of the little book.[12] John's next teacher wasn't an improvement. An elderly discharged solder from Fort Dearborn was hired to instruct the children at the settlement. But the old man proved to be a drunk, and he was either inebriated in front of his students or simply did not show up at all.[13]

Educational opportunities in Detroit were a haphazard affair. Common schools, or public schools, which taught basic skills such as reading and writing, came and went with the passing year. One school, run by a Mr. Payne, was noted for its classical instruction of Latin and Greek. Perhaps the most notable was the school run by a Mr. Danforth, who was known for a violent temper and for throwing things, including knives, at his students.[14] Whether John Jr. attended any of these schools is unknown.

During these years John Kinzie Jr. developed a natural talent for picking up Native languages. By the time he was fifteen he was already fluent in Potawatomi, Ottawa, and Dakota dialects. His general education must have been sufficient, for when he was sixteen, his father used his connections with the American Fur Company to get his son a position as clerk at Mackinac Island.

Following in his father's footsteps, John Kinzie Jr. entered the fur trade in 1818 as an apprentice to Robert Stuart, a Scotsman and one of the principals of the American Fur Company. The American Fur Company was the brainchild of John Jacob Astor, a native of Germany who immigrated to the United States in 1783. Astor started out as a baker, but his shrewd

A sketch of Mackinac Island by David Bate Douglas, ca. 1820, at the time John Kinzie lived there. GREENSLADE SPECIAL COLLECTIONS AND ARCHIVES, KENYON COLLEGE, GAMBIER, OHIO (99-024)

business acumen soon led him to various ventures before he struck out into the fur trade. Based out of New York, Astor attempted to develop an independent fur trading colony called Astoria at the mouth of the Columbia River in Oregon. Though that venture had failed by 1818, Astor had steadily expanded his business operations elsewhere and had amassed a business empire that was quickly becoming a monopoly. Astor wielded considerable political power with many sympathetic politicians, including Lewis Cass, the territorial governor of Michigan. Astor's company controlled the fur trade throughout the Great Lakes region from the company's Northern Department, based out of Mackinac Island.[15] The island was ideally situated in the middle of the Straits of Mackinac, which connected Lake Michigan and Lake Huron.

Robert Stuart, Kinzie Jr.'s boss, had a long association with the American Fur Company and its owner, going as far back as Astor's efforts in Oregon. Stuart was no stranger to living in the wilderness, and he undertook an extremely dangerous trek back east when the Astoria colony failed. Stuart rose to become one of Astor's most trusted lieutenants, along with Ramsay Crooks. Together Stuart and Crooks ran the Northern Department.

New faces were common at a place like Mackinac Island, as traders and new employees came and went. Among them was a young man named Gordon Hubbard, on his first journey into the wilderness. Hubbard had left his home in Vermont, determined to strike out into the fur trade. Hubbard and Kinzie became fast friends. Most clerks, including Hubbard, were assigned to brigades, or groups of canoes traveling together to transport fur packs and supplies across the Great Lakes and the inland

Portrait of Ramsay Crooks. WHI IMAGE ID 2593

waters. But Kinzie, who had made a favorable impression on his employers almost from the time he had arrived, was stationed at Mackinac Island and boarded with the Stuart family.[16]

The operations on the island were vast. Fort Michilimackinac dominated the island, situated high on a bluff overlooking the town. By the time Kinzie lived there, the island had become home to the regional government, the regional court, and a major military installation and was a major base for the fur trade. The American Fur Company maintained a number of warehouses and offices and a store there. The island served as

A modern-day photograph of the American Fur Company Store on Mackinac Island; John Kinzie worked as a clerk overseeing operations here. COURTESY OF THE AUTHOR

headquarters for the company's operations not only in the Great Lakes, but for the western US territories as well.

Traders in the field sent bundles of fur pelts to the warehouses on Mackinac, where the furs were sorted and rebundled, and then shipped to markets in the east. Kinzie worked in these warehouses. Sorting the furs could be tedious; the task could start as early as 5 a.m. and continue as late as 7 p.m., with counting and recounting necessary if a discrepancy was found.[17] Stuart demanded an exacting schedule of his clerks. When Kinzie wasn't counting furs or at his desk filling out ledgers and other paperwork, he was back in the warehouse supervising the numerous engages, or hired laborers; receiving packs of furs; and assembling the tools, trade goods, and equipment, or "outfits," the traders used for their trips into the wilderness.[18]

While at Mackinac, Kinzie continued his education. He read aloud to Mrs. Stuart every evening, and he practiced his letters under the exacting tutelage of Mr. Stuart, who could display extreme cruelty and remarkable tenderness with ease, a personality trait that was perhaps reflective of his hard life on the frontier. As Kinzie's good friend Hubbard recalled years later:

On one occasion, when he [Kinzie] had finished making out a long invoice, when he had taken unusual care to write nicely and in commercial shape, and supposed he would be highly complimented on its production, delivered it to Mr. Stewart, who carefully looked it over, sheet after sheet, and on the very last page discovered a blot and a figure erased and rewritten. Pointing to them with a scowl, he said, "Do you call that well done? Go and do it over"; and he tore it into fragments. Poor John was sorely mortified, but was consoled by Mrs. Stewart, who had been instructed to do so by her husband, and proceeded to rewrite his invoice, satisfied either of his own imperfections, or the disagreeable temper of his master.[19]

Stuart was full of lessons for his young clerk. On another occasion, Kinzie was found to be increasingly insolent to an old voyageur who was working as a servant in the Stuarts' household. Kinzie preferred to order the old man about rather than asking him politely to do things. The old man complained to Stuart, who agreed: "You are right, old man. The boy is foolish; he should always treat an old man with respect; give him a good thrashing the next time he insults you." Stuart then orchestrated an incident that resulted in a fistfight between the voyageur and the boy. Stuart watched from an upstairs room as his clerk learned a lesson in respecting his elders regardless of their station.[20]

On another occasion, when Kinzie was overseeing a team of employees hauling wood over the ice from a nearby island, he became impatient with his men's slow pace. Seizing the reins, Kinzie led the team back to Mackinac Island in record time. Stuart, however, was not amused. The Scotsman believed that a good businessman was methodical and never departed from routine, and thus Kinzie's reward was to haul wood across the ice for the remainder of the winter.

Kinzie's duties were varied while on the island. But there was still some time for leisure. Since water was the principal form of travel, and communication to and from the island was cut off during the cold months, winter could be long and tedious. Kinzie found time to hunt foxes, and he

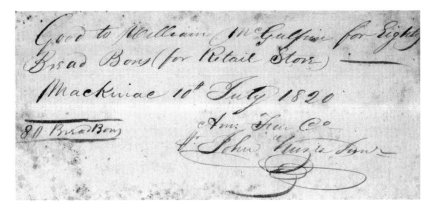

A voucher issued by John Kinzie while working in the American Fur Company Store on Mackinac Island. NEWBERRY LIBRARY

learned to play the violin from an unknown woman of mixed ancestry. He would continue to play for the rest of his life, often pulling out his fiddle to entertain guests at Fort Winnebago and years later in Chicago.

Two years into his apprenticeship, Kinzie was assigned as a clerk to the company store. By the end of his apprenticeship, he had earned enough confidence from his employers that he was placed in charge of the store and occasionally was assigned temporary clerks to work for him, including his friend Hubbard.[21]

The store, which catered to voyageurs, soldiers, and officers from the fort, was often a dramatic place to be. On June 6, 1822, Kinzie was working in the store during a particularly busy stretch with many customers. That day, a voyageur for the American Fur Company named Alexis St. Martin was loitering in the store with fellow engages. Standing next to St. Martin was a man carrying a firearm loaded with buckshot. Inexplicably, the gun accidentally discharged and shot St. Martin in the abdomen. The injury was thought to be fatal, but Dr. William Beaumont, the post surgeon, arrived within thirty minutes and was able to stabilize the wound. St. Martin would survive, but he was left with a semipermanent hole in his abdomen. Beaumont seized the opportunity and used the wound to explore the workings of the stomach. On and off for the next ten years, Beaumont studied St. Martin and the gastric juices extracted from his stomach, resulting in groundbreaking research into the human digestive system.[22]

When Kinzie's apprenticeship ended in 1823, he was hired on as a clerk for the company. Though his duties would remain the same, he was now a full-fledged employee. But his scenery was about to change. Later that year, Kinzie was sent southwest to Prairie du Chien, to assist Joseph Rolette in the fur trade along the Mississippi River.

3

Prairie du Chien

Joseph Rolette was a clever yet pompous French Canadian who had been working the fur trade in Prairie du Chien for almost twenty years.[1] One year after Kinzie arrived, his younger brother Robert joined him as a clerk. Kinzie's time in Prairie du Chien may have been his introduction to the Ho-Chunk language, possibly from Nicholas Boilvin, an experienced local fur trader and Indian agent. Kinzie had also mastered Ojibwe by this time, and within two years of arriving at the Mississippi River, he had compiled a dictionary of the Ho-Chunk language. It's unclear why Kinzie undertook such a project. Perhaps Stuart or his partner Ramsay Crooks felt such an exercise was useful, or perhaps Kinzie was operating on his own initiative. Regardless, the document was extensive, containing a list of seventy-four terms and organized by phrases, verbs, nouns, pronouns, conjunctions, adverbs, and numbers. The document also contained the words and music to several songs.[2]

Not all of Kinzie's activities in Prairie du Chien were confined to the fur trade or learning local Native culture. A year after his arrival, he became involved in an effort to establish a Sunday school. Julianna Lockwood, the wife of a local fur trader, was aghast to find no religious instruction of any kind on Sundays. So she took it upon herself to remedy the matter. Lockwood enlisted the aid of three supporters—a young woman by the name of Crawford, Fort Crawford surgeon Dr. Edwin James, and Kinzie—to organize the school in the spring of 1825. Initially Rolette resisted their efforts; he apparently objected to the school because he didn't think of the idea first. Lockwood was a Protestant, and Rolette played on the religious fears of the village inhabitants, many of whom were Roman Catholic.

Eventually the matter blew over once the school accepted both Catholic and Protestant children.[3] Kinzie's own religious beliefs at the time are not known. That religion was important to him was evidenced by his activities at Prairie du Chien, but it is also possible that his religious views were cemented later after he married Juliette, who was Episcopalian.[4]

—◦❚❘❘◦—

In the summer of 1825, the largest treaty council in the upper Mississippi up to that date convened at Prairie du Chien. For miles above and below the village, tents and campsites dotted the bluffs. Unlike most treaty councils, which were designed to get land cessions from the Indians, this one was an attempt by federal officials to solve a number long-standing problems plaguing the upper Mississippi Valley frontier. Among these problems were the continued loyalty of the region's tribes to Great Britain, the smuggling of British trade goods into the area, the constant state of warfare between the Dakota and the Ojibwe, and the increasing trespass of lead miners onto Indian lands.[5]

Many of the region's tribes still held a nominal allegiance to Great Britain, and British flags could often be found in Indian villages across Wisconsin and Minnesota. In the years immediately following the War of 1812, US policy wasn't yet focused on the mass removal of tribes from Wisconsin and instead was designed to simply pacify the local tribes and to shift regional control from the British. The war's impact on federal Indian policy, and on federal policy in general, cannot be underestimated.

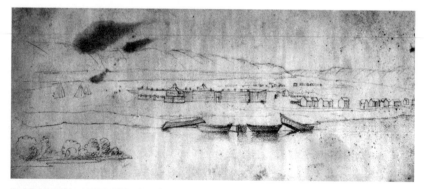

Prairie du Chien, 1829. This sketch was drawn about five years after Kinzie left; it would have looked very similar when he lived here. WHI IMAGE ID 42293

For most of the war's duration, the United States had suffered a string of defeats. Washington, DC, had been captured and burned. The northeastern states had considered secession. Only at the war's end did Americans experience any significant victories; consequently a wave of nationalism swept the country following the war. Anglophobia permeated the political class, including a rising political star, Andrew Jackson.

The council at Prairie du Chien was in part about national security. The peace treaty ending the war required the British to abandon all forts in American territory. In the western Great Lakes, the British evacuated Mackinac and other posts but established a new one on Drummonds Island, not far away on Lake Huron, and a second one at Malden just across the river from Detroit.[6] The closeness of British army forts fueled American paranoia that their old enemy could still influence area tribes—a sentiment that guided federal Indian policy in the years following the war. In reality, US officials had little to fear. British Indian policy was in shambles following the War of 1812. London had little interest in Indian affairs on the Great Lakes, and local British officials struggled to maintain relationships with tribes who now lived within US territory.[7]

National anti-British feelings also had something to do with the primary economic driver of the region, the fur trade. In the years following the War of 1812, John Jacob Astor was in the midst of expanding his control of the fur trade throughout the Great Lakes. He had successfully convinced the federal government that his activities were an extension of national interests. If he controlled the trade, he helped keep Britain at bay.[8]

But the smuggling of trade goods was a never-ending problem that posed a direct threat to the politically powerful American Fur Company. At the end of the war, British trading companies moved their posts outside of American territory, but they continued to trade with tribes living within the US. British trade goods were coming into the region, and valuable fur pelts were going out.

The combined concerns over national security and the desires of the American Fur Company were certainly enough for federal officials to convene a council, but even more pressing issues threatened the lives of anyone living in the upper Mississippi River valley. In Minnesota, the Ojibwe and the Dakota had been embroiled in a bitter and bloody border war for years. By 1825, this constant state of warfare threatened to spill over into neighboring tribes, including the Ho-Chunk, who were allied with the Dakota.

Another emerging problem for the United States was the rapidly growing mining population. During the nineteenth century, lead had many important uses, including for shot, paint, medicine, and window frames. During the Revolutionary War, the struggling colonies suffered a constant shortage of the ore, and afterward the new republic perpetually relied upon Great Britain for its supply.[9] But there were some sources within US boundaries. For years Americans had been extracting lead from fields in eastern Missouri. The old French community of St. Genevieve was the center of such activities.[10] The Missouri fields were for a time the greatest single source of lead for the young United States.

The peace treaties signed in the summer of 1816 established a small, five-square-mile reservation for mining lead by a confederation of Ottawa, Potawatomi, and Ojibwe (collectively referred to at the time as the Illinois tribes), who controlled a narrow strip of territory on the east bank of the Mississippi in northwestern Illinois and southwestern Wisconsin. But the specific location of the reservation was left undefined. The president of the United States was supposed to determine the site once the precise location of the lead mines was identified. Eventually the reservation was located along the Fever River at the present-day site of Galena, Illinois. As small as this plot of land was, it was the first toehold Americans had in the Wisconsin and Illinois lead region.[11]

Before long the reservation along the Fever River began to attract miners. The high demand for the grey ore lured those hoping for a sure way to make a fortune. Access to the mines, however, wasn't easy. Since 1807 the federal government had retained rights to all mineral lands in its possession. A prospective miner had to sign a lease, usually for five years, in order to legally operate mines. This had the effect of creating small, loosely organized settlements, as miners had no choice but to stick to the little plots they leased.[12]

In the beginning most of the mining operations were largely confined to the Fever River near present-day Galena, Illinois. Many early prospectors simply traded with the local Indians for the ore. Miners soon discovered, however, that more deposits could be found to the north in the Michigan Territory, in what is now southwestern Wisconsin. In fact, 90 percent of all the lead ore found in the lead region would be discovered on lands now within the state of Wisconsin.[13]

Ten years after the end of the War of 1812, mining operations could be found not only on the Fever River but also on the Apple River to the south and the Sinsinawa River to the north.[14] The Sinsinawa flowed from lands in the Michigan Territory, and with a steady determination the miners were working their way farther from the Mississippi River and deeper into Ho-Chunk territory.[15]

There was a problem, however. The mineral resources beyond the Fever River were on lands not owned by the United States. The land belonged to the Ho-Chunk. And the Ho-Chunk did not want miners on their property. In fact, they didn't want anything to do with the Americans at all. In January 1820, Captain William Whistler, a captain in the Third Infantry stationed at Fort Howard, Green Bay, experienced firsthand the indifference and animosity of the Wisconsin tribe during a trip down the Fox River:

> As I was passing a village of the Winnebago Indians, situated at the entrance of the Winnebago Lake, my boat was fired on by a party of that tribe, who were assembled on the shore. I immediately ordered my boat to stop, and directed my Interpreter to enquire the cause of this unexpected attack on the American flag, which was hoisted on my approach to the Village, in reply I was given to understand, that they commanded the passage, & required all boats to stop & report to them.[16]

Whistler was not the only army officer to have problems with the Ho-Chunk. Only a few months after Whistler's incident along the Fox River, two US soldiers were murdered by Ho-Chunk warriors at Fort Armstrong on Rock Island. The soldiers belonged to the Fifth Infantry commanded by Colonel Henry Leavenworth. Leavenworth wanted to strongly chastise the Ho-Chunk, going as far as enlisting the Sauk and Meskwaki to assist him in hunting down the culprits. Only after Indian agent Lawrence Taliaferro intervened did Leavenworth decide to insist on hostages and negotiations. Eventually the combination of negotiations and threatened action persuaded the Ho-Chunk leaders to surrender the murderers.[17]

These two incidents are noteworthy because they not only clearly show that the Ho-Chunk were not impressed with US power, but they also illustrate the temperament of the Ho-Chunk Nation in the years immediately following the War of 1812. Mathew Irwin, who ran the government trading house at Green Bay, was perhaps thinking of these two incidents when he wrote in 1820, "No other tribe seems to possess so much jealousy of the whites, and such reluctance to have intercourse with them, as this."[18] Irwin went on to say, "They will suffer no encroachment upon their soil; nor any persons to pass through it, without giving a satisfactory explanation of their motives and intentions. In failing to comply with this preliminary step, their lives would be in danger."[19]

In the summer of 1825, President Monroe appointed Lewis Cass and William Clark to hold the great council at Prairie du Chien in an effort to resolve many of these matters. The old trading settlement was chosen because all the Native peoples considered it a neutral ground. Anyone could go there without fear of attack. The council would be the largest gathering of Indians on the upper Mississippi anyone had ever seen.[20] Official documents detailing treaty negotiations do not make any mention of Kinzie, nor does the treaty list him as a witness, but given the size of the event and the obvious impact it would have on the Indian trade, it's impossible to imagine him not present.

Though the issue of British loyalty and smuggling was important, the bulk of the council focused on tribal boundaries. The commissioners believed the war between the Ojibwe and the Dakota was the result of neither tribe having a clearly defined territorial boundary line. The simple solution was to draw a line everyone could agree on. Any tribe with lands adjoining either faction would need to have their boundaries determined as well; as a result, the treaty attempted to establish boundary lines between all the region's tribes, including the Ho-Chunk.

The problem for Cass and Clark was that the Indians themselves did not recognize the concept of boundary lines. This point was perhaps best made by the Ho-Chunk chief Caramaunee:

The lands I claim are mine the nations here know it is not only claimed by us but by our brothers the Sac & Fox [Meskwaki], Menominee, Iowa, Ottowa & Sioux [Dakota] they have [used] it in common it

would be difficult to divide it. It belongs as much to one as the other
... I did not know that any of my nation had any particular land—It
is true every one owns his own lodge & the ground he may cultivate I
had thought the rivers were the common property of all Red Skins &
not used exclusively by any particular nation.[21]

At the treaty council, the commissioners would propose a boundary
line, and one chief and then another would reject it. As the hot and humid
days of August wore on, Cass and Clark sensed they were getting nowhere.
Finally, in frustration, the two commissioners told the chiefs that they
alone could decide where the boundaries would be drawn. The Indian
leaders went into separate councils and drew their own boundary lines.

This method applied to the Ho-Chunk as it did to everyone else. They
were present at the council not only because of their proximity to the Dakota, but also because of their growing discontent over the trespassing
of the miners. Ho-Chunk territory bordered with the Illinois tribes (the
Ottawa, Potawatomi, and Ojibwe), and together they effectively controlled
all of the lands of the lead region.

The treaty council at Prairie du Chien, as illustrated by James Otto Lewis. Kinzie attended
two councils at Prairie du Chien, including this one in 1825. WHI IMAGE ID 3142

At the council meeting, the Ho-Chunk and the Illinois tribes met separately and created a boundary line that would divide their people as well as the lead region. Unfortunately, it was a vague line, one that is difficult, even today, to clearly draw on a map. It was probably clear to the Ho-Chunk and the Ottawa, Potawatomi, and Ojibwe where the boundary line was, but that didn't matter if the miners, the army, and the Indian agents couldn't see it on a map. In the end, no one could say they knew where the boundary line ran. Prior to the treaty, the lands around the Fever River mines were seen as held in common by all the tribes. Now a vague boundary, almost impossible to interpret, was imposed on the region. Trespassing onto Ho-Chunk land had become inevitable.

It is possible that Kinzie renewed his acquaintance with Lewis Cass during this council meeting. In addition to being an old friend of the Kinzie family, Cass was a loyal supporter of John Jacob Astor and more than a passing acquaintance with Kinzie's employers at Mackinac. Cass must have taken note of Kinzie's studies of the Ho-Chunk language. As superintendent of Indian affairs, Cass constantly encouraged his agents to gather as much ethnographic data on the surrounding tribes as possible. Either that summer or by the fall, Cass offered Kinzie a position as one of his secretaries.

The appointment came none too soon, for young Kinzie had found himself in a rather delicate situation. A few months after the treaty council, in the fall of 1825, Kinzie came down with malaria, a disease that can bring on intense fever and severe pain. Four Legs, a prominent Ho-Chunk chief of a village at the northern end of Lake Winnebago, came into a local store to trade. When he heard that Kinzie was sick, Four Legs immediately went to him to express his sympathy and perhaps to suggest an appropriate medicine. In the course of conversation, Four Legs mentioned how sad it was for Kinzie to be in such a state without a wife to attend him. Four Legs pointed out that he had a lovely daughter, "handsome and healthy, a capital nurse, the best hand in all the tribe at trapping beaver and musk-rats." Four Legs promised he would bring her with him on his return trip the following spring.[22]

Kinzie, in a state of agony, agreed, simply to get the old man to go away. Several months later, Four Legs returned with his daughter. The name of this young woman unfortunately has been lost; in Juliette's later writings,

Chief Four Legs, in an illustration ca. 1835. WHI IMAGE ID 26879

she refers to her only as "Miss Four Legs." The young woman was carrying a large pack of furs. Upon meeting Kinzie, she threw the pack at his feet. It was a symbolic gesture, one that symbolized their new relationship.

Kinzie, aghast, had completely forgotten the conversation of the previous months. He took her furs and tried to pay her with a shirt and some beads. Four Legs finally confronted Kinzie. "Well, I have brought you my daughter, according to our agreement," he said. "How do you like her?"

Kinzie noted she was indeed a fine woman and would certainly make an excellent wife to someone else, but that regrettably he had just received an appointment by Governor Cass to live among the Wyandot in Ohio. It simply would not be fair to Four Legs's daughter, Kinzie told him, to marry a man who may not return to the region for years, if ever. After some additional haggling, Kinzie was able to buy his way out of the agreement, although years later he would not admit even to Juliette just how much he'd had to pay to convince the chief to let the matter drop.[23]

Kinzie left Prairie du Chien in the spring of 1826. His new boss, Lewis Cass, took advantage of Kinzie's skills as a linguist and sent him to the Upper Sandusky region of Ohio to live among the Wyandot and learn their language and their customs. We don't know exactly where Kinzie lived during this period. Most likely he stayed near or around the Piqua agency under the direction of Indian agent John Johnston, who was compiling his own notes on the language of the Shawnee.[24]

The Piqua agency was a comfortable place to be. Johnston had been a factor before he retired to be a gentleman farmer in northwestern Ohio. Factors were government-sponsored fur traders, part of a program once designed to offer an alternative to the American Fur Company. But Astor considered the factor system a direct threat to his monopolistic hold on the fur trade, and he used his extensive political influence to have the system abolished in 1822. By the time Johnston received his appointment as Indian agent in 1818, he had established a successful farm that included a spacious three-story brick farmhouse, a two-story brick spring house, and other outbuildings. Kinzie spent almost a year in Ohio gathering information and ultimately drafting a 229-page dictionary of the Wyandot language and an 8-page report on the customs of the Wyandot.[25]

By the summer of 1827, Kinzie had returned to Detroit, where he found Cass in the midst of preparations for another council. This gathering was a continuation of the work that began at the council at Prairie du Chien in 1825. At the 1825 council, many of the tribes had not been completely represented, which had created major obstacles for the commissioners. The Menominee, for example, had sent only a small delegation, which meant the boundary lines in eastern Wisconsin were left incomplete. Cass had traveled to the western reaches of Lake Superior in 1826, to the site of modern-day Duluth, to continue his work establishing the northern boundaries for all the region's tribes. Now he was back, intending to hold a final council at Little Butte des Morts, a lake on the Fox River just north of Lake Winnebago near the present-day cities of Neenah and Menasha.[26]

Upon arrival in Green Bay, however, Cass found he had other matters to deal with first. As Cass stepped off the boat he was handed an express dispatch from John Marsh, the Indian subagent at Prairie du Chien. Red Bird, a chief of the Ho-Chunk Nation, had attacked a family of mixed ancestry, living just south of the village. Warriors from Red Bird's village had also attacked two keelboats on the Mississippi several miles to the north, and messengers had been sent to other Ho-Chunk villages to encourage an all-out war.

4

THE WINNEBAGO WAR OF 1827

The Ho-Chunk entered the nineteenth century a strong yet divided tribe. It was a different story one hundred years earlier. The tribe had begun the eighteenth century a nearly extinguished people caught between the warring Meskwaki and the French, enduring epidemics and internal divisions. By the time of the French and Indian War, the Ho-Chunk had broken into two distinct bands. One group lived along the Rock River, which runs from south-central Wisconsin through northwestern Illinois and eventually connects with the Mississippi. A second group (sometimes referred to as the Green Bay Band) was concentrated along the Fox River between Lake Winnebago and Green Bay.

The American Revolution only reaffirmed the growing disparity among the Ho-Chunk. Following the capture of Vincennes in 1779, George Rodgers Clark followed his military success with a diplomatic coup when he negotiated a peace treaty with the Rock River Ho-Chunk. Not every faction of the tribe remained out of the war, however. The Green Bay Band continued to support Great Britain and participated in several campaigns, often serving under Charles de Langlade.[1]

With the Treaty of Paris in 1783 ending the revolution, the land that would later become Wisconsin passed into the jurisdiction of the United States, but it was difficult for the Ho-Chunk and many other area tribes to come to terms with American authority. The British remained a strong presence in the region, and it wasn't long before the Ho-Chunk reestablished a relationship with their old fur-trading partners. The defeat of the Western Confederacy (a coalition of more than two dozen tribes dominated by Shawnee and Miami) at the Battle of Fallen Timbers; the

Ho-Chunk Lands in 1825 and Today

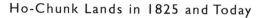

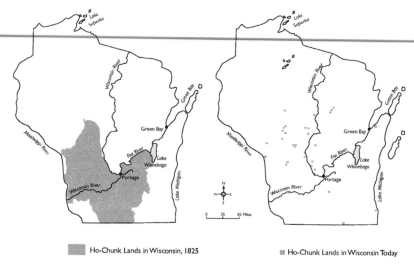

Ho-Chunk Lands in Wisconsin, 1825   ■ Ho-Chunk Lands in Wisconsin Today

UNIVERSITY OF WISCONSIN CARTOGRAPHY LAB

subsequent Treaty of Greenville, in which much of present-day Ohio was ceded to the United States; and the expansion of settlements in Illinois and the Mississippi River Valley further alienated the Ho-Chunk from the United States.[2]

By the early nineteenth century, the Ho-Chunk Nation was experiencing a period of relative peace and stability marked by a rise in population and could claim much of what is today southwest and central Wisconsin. Tribal territory stretched from the Fox River Valley near their historic homelands on Green Bay, westward to the Mississippi, to the headwaters of the Black River in north-central Wisconsin, and as far south as the Rock River in Illinois.[3] Tribal economy depended on maple sugar production, lead mining, and the fur trade. For the Ho-Chunk, who controlled so much of the lead-bearing lands in the upper Mississippi River Valley, lead was a particularly important trading commodity that helped counter poor crop harvests or lean hunting seasons.[4]

At the outbreak of war in 1812 between the United States and Great Britain, the Ho-Chunk aligned themselves with the British. The tribe helped to defeat the Americans on the Great Lakes early in the war; participated in most of the far-western campaigns, including operations against Detroit and Fort Meigs; and helped with the seizure of Mackinac Island. Later in the war, as American forces returned to the region, the Ho-Chunk fought with the British at the Battle of Prairie du Chien and the Battle of the Thames.

By war's end, however, the Ho-Chunk would be forsaken by their British allies. The Treaty of Ghent, negotiated by diplomats in Europe, re-affirmed American claims to the western Great Lakes once and for all. The treaty also required that all Indian lands and possessions be returned to their prewar status. Although there was no stipulation for the enforcement of the treaty, in the end the British withdrew from American territory. This outcome surprised and disgusted almost everyone in the region, es-pecially the British traders. The Ho-Chunk and other regional tribes were disillusioned and angered by what they perceived as a betrayal by their former allies. In a council held at Mackinac Island in June 1815, Zazaman-iga, or Walks Naked, a brother of Four Legs, expressed the feelings of the Ho-Chunk:

> Father!—You promised repeatedly, that this place would not be given up; and if you actually intend to abandon us to our inveterate enemy, who always sought our destruction, it would be better that you kill us at once, rather than expose us to a lingering death. It is probable that the Americans may not at first show their intentions of destroying us immediately; but we are fully persuaded that they will avail them-selves of the first opportunity for exterminating us. Father!—The peace made between you and the Big Knives, may be a lasting one; but it cannot be for us, for we hate them; they so often deceived us that we cannot put any faith in them.[5]

The Ho-Chunk signed a peace treaty of sorts with the Americans the following year. However, only the band from Green Bay participated.[6] In fact, as part of the treaty, the Green Bay Band agreed to have no further contact with their Rock River brethren until the Americans signed a sep-arate peace treaty with them. Yet that peace treaty seems never to have happened. The Rock River Ho-Chunk remained opposed to any American presence, and leaders of that band circulated from village to village, urging a continuation of hostilities.

When the US Army arrived to take control of Green Bay in 1816, officers were apprehensive over the reception they would receive from the Ho-Chunk. However, the newly arrived garrison had little to worry about, as the predominant feeling among the area Ho-Chunk was peaceful; but the failure of federal authorities to reach out to the entire tribe not only perpetuated the smoldering resentment among some, it also cemented two distinct tribal factions capable of making significant decisions mutually exclusive of each other. In the following years other factions would emerge within the Ho-Chunk tribe, including villages near the portage of the Fox and Wisconsin Rivers, and a new band living just north of Prairie du Chien.[7]

In the years immediately following the War of 1812, the United States wanted to reaffirm its authority in the western Great Lakes and the upper Mississippi River Valley. The federal government established new forts there, including Fort Crawford at Prairie du Chien and Fort Armstrong at Rock Island, and rebuilt Fort Dearborn in Chicago. Each of these posts included an Indian agency nearby.

But within ten years, federal priorities had shifted. General Jacob Brown, the commanding general of the army, believed that by concentrating a large number of infantry near St. Louis, soldiers could then be available for immediate dispatch whenever they were needed along the northwestern frontier. The newly established infantry school at the Jefferson Barracks at St. Louis was created for this purpose, along with the laudable ideal of providing continued training, especially for officers who tended to languish at the small, isolated posts.[8] By 1826 army leadership believed that Fort Crawford, at Prairie du Chien, had outlived its usefulness and ordered its garrison to relocate upriver to Fort Snelling, in modern-day St. Paul, Minnesota. But closing the fort also eliminated the only effective police force in the upper Mississippi Valley.

In March 1826, on the eve of the garrison's departure, a family of mixed ancestry was found murdered in their burned-out cabin about six miles north of Prairie du Chien, on the Iowa side of the Mississippi River. The Francis Methode family, new arrivals to the area, had been harvesting maple sugar that spring. News of their deaths quickly spread through the Prairie du Chien settlement, and suspicion fell almost immediately upon the Ho-Chunk, although some believed that perhaps a Sauk war party had killed the family.[9] Troops from Fort Crawford searched the area and discovered a trail of debris leading from the family's cabin to a small Ho-Chunk winter village nearby.[10]

The commander of Fort Crawford, Colonel Morgan, concluded that because of the close proximity of the Ho-Chunk camp and the fact that the Mississippi was partly thawed and partly covered with broken ice, making river crossing extremely difficult, the family must have been attacked and killed by members of the Ho-Chunk tribe.[11]

Local Ho-Chunk leaders were summoned to the fort, where officers demanded they surrender the murderers. According to Morgan, the chiefs, accompanied by eighty members of the tribe, converged on Prairie du Chien. In a letter to the adjutant general in St. Louis, Morgan wrote, "They at first pressed me to name the persons whom I supposed to be guilty; but this I refused to do, telling the chiefs that they must themselves know the guilty and these they must surrender."[12] Admitting that it may indeed have been a member of their tribe who killed the family, the Ho-Chunk leaders said they were unable to identify who the perpetrators were. Some leaders even professed the tribe was completely innocent in the matter.[13]

Exasperated, Morgan took drastic measures. Faced with the uncooperative Ho-Chunk, and believing he had irrefutable evidence of their culpability, Morgan followed the advice of James Duane Doty, the presiding judge of the Additional Court of Michigan Territory, and arrested six tribal members, using them as hostages in the hopes that the arrests would induce the tribe to give up the guilty persons.[14]

After several days, and under duress, tribal leaders gave several names to the authorities in Prairie du Chien. Almost a dozen Indians were arrested and held at Fort Crawford. However, many of those arrested believed they would not be held for any extended length of time because of lack of direct proof. Colonel Morgan agreed. He concluded that the only other course of action he had left was to punish the Ho-Chunk economically by revoking all trade licenses with the tribe, or resort to outright warfare.[15] But he would not have time to try either tactic. By October the fort garrison and its colonel had abandoned the post.

Instead, a court of inquiry was held by Nicholas Boilvin, who was not only the Indian agent but also the local justice of the peace.[16] Evidence was slim. Despite the debris trail leading to the Ho-Chunk village, there were no surviving witnesses to the murders, and the Ho-Chunk people were unwilling to cooperate by offering additional information. Ultimately, the case against many of the defendants fell apart, and all but two were released from custody. When the garrison was withdrawn to Fort Snelling, the two prisoners were taken with them.

—II—

The two prisoners taken to Fort Snelling would unknowingly play a pivotal role in the fate of the Ho-Chunk Nation. The Treaty of 1825 at Prairie du Chien had brokered a peace between the Dakota and the Ojibwe, but it was a fragile peace destined not to last. In May of 1826, as the turmoil of the Methode murders started to pass, both the Dakota and the Ojibwe were invited to Fort Snelling to receive their annual gifts from Lawrence Taliaferro, the local Indian agent.

Taliaferro arranged for the principal leaders of both tribes to attend an evening feast to reaffirm the peace accord signed in 1825. The evening was filled with celebrations, eating, and speech making. As the Dakota leaders departed, and for reasons still unclear, several members of their party fired muskets into the Ojibwe camp. At least one Ojibwe was killed, and many others suffered terrible, crippling wounds.

Action from the army came swiftly. Colonel Josiah Snelling, commander of Fort Snelling, feared a reprisal from the Ojibwe and sent a detachment to the nearest Dakota village to round up as many warriors as could be had. Thirty men were taken and thrown into the fort's guardhouse. Early the next morning, Colonel Snelling brought several of the wounded survivors into the fort to identify the culprits, and two were singled out. Snelling, "washing his hands of the matter," turned the men over to the Ojibwe, who summarily shot them. Snelling insisted the bodies were not to remain on or near the boundaries of the post, and the Ojibwe obliged by throwing the slain men into the Mississippi River.[17]

The animosity between the Ojibwe and the Dakota was always brewing trouble, but now the Dakota living near Fort Snelling had reason to focus their anger toward the United States. Thoughts of the death of two of their warriors festered among tribal leaders for nearly a year. Unwilling to openly attack the Americans, the Dakota turned to an old ally, the Ho-Chunk, who at the time were holding a council at a nearby village to discuss the situation of the trespassing miners.[18] The Dakota relayed the story of the murders at Fort Snelling, but they added a twist—that American soldiers at the fort had shot the two Ho-Chunk prisoners.[19]

Present at the Ho-Chunk council was Waunigsootshkau, or Red Bird, so named for the two stuffed red-colored birds he wore on both shoulders. Biographical information on Red Bird is scarce, but he was considered both a civil and war chief of the Prairie LaCrosse Band of Ho-Chunk. The Dakota chiefs found an opportunity in Red Bird, who had recently returned from a failed attack on the Ojibwe.[20] Accounts are sketchy, but apparently the Dakotas in council claimed Red Bird had failed his tribe in war, and his tribe was allowing Americans to overrun their land. Now two of their tribe had been murdered, and again the guilty were going unpunished. Red Bird, the Dakota leaders cried, must take revenge.[21]

It is difficult to ascertain with certainty whether the Dakota were really this instrumental in instigating a Ho-Chunk attack. However, a year later, during the Council of 1828 at Green Bay, Ho-Chunk chief Hoo-Wan-ne-ka, or Little Elk, would comment, "What happened last year did not come from us. Our brothers (the Sioux) [Dakota] pushed us on, and we were fools enough to believe them."[22]

At first Red Bird was reluctant to attack Americans living in the area. Prairie du Chien, the nearest white settlement, was a familiar community. He had friends there. One account even claims that Red Bird went as far as making a phony attack on the settlement.[23] This did not satisfy the leaders of his tribe. Now he was called a "coward." Red Bird grew increasingly agitated and humiliated. Finally he could take it no more. He would avenge the murders at Fort Snelling and punish the Americans living above the Rock River.[24]

Red Bird surrounded himself with men he knew well and traveled to Prairie du Chien. He was accompanied by his son, Wekaw, or The Sun, and Little Buffalo, a brother-in-law. In a community still dominated by a population of mixed French and Indian ancestry, seeking out Americans was not easy. Red Bird's party first went to the James Lockwood house, the home of the only American family at the settlement. But Lockwood had just left the day before on a journey to New York.[25] Red Bird also sought out the local Indian agent, John Marsh, possibly intending to kill him as well, but to no avail.

Red Bird, in an illustration ca. 1848. WHI IMAGE ID 3911

Running out of options, Red Bird settled on two cabins located at Mc-Nair's coulee, a valley two miles below Prairie du Chien near the Wisconsin River.[26] There, in a one-room log cabin on a ridge at the entrance to the coulee, resided the family of Rejiste Gagnier, whose father was French and mother African American.[27] Gagnier's wife, Theresa, was of French and Dakota parentage. They had a young son and an infant daughter. The family ran a small farm with the help of a hired hand, an old discharged American soldier named Solomon Lipcap.

On the surface it may seem strange that Red Bird chose a mixed-ancestry homestead on the outskirts of town as the target for his attack. However, the Gagnier farm was located next to a lot owned by another American, Thomas McNair. It is possible that Red Bird, unable to find Marsh or Lockwood, went searching for McNair only to discover the Gagnier homestead, where Lipcap, the American, was working as a field hand.[28]

Gagnier and Red Bird knew each other, and it was not an unusual practice to take visitors into one's home and serve them a meal. As the three men entered the homestead, they were joined by a twelve-year-old neighbor boy, Pascal Menard. Accounts vary as to what happened next. Some say the Indians sat for a while. Others claim an argument began almost immediately. Menard later recalled that Red Bird's son tried to take away Gagnier's firearms. Red Bird himself was apparently staring out the cabin window as if contemplating something, but then turned and shot Gagnier in the chest. Lipcap suffered a more severe fate. He was beaten with the butt of Wekaw's gun, taken outside, then chased down, stabbed, and scalped to death.

Young Menard dove out a cabin window and took cover behind a nearby hill. One of the warriors made a move for Mrs. Gagnier, who broke away, grabbed a rifle, and leveled it at the intruders. Grabbing her son, she made a quick escape out of the building and ran to the village for help. Left behind in the scuffle was her eleven-month-old daughter, who was later found scalped and badly cut.[29] Amazingly, the little girl survived, badly mutilated though she was, and became a bit of a curiosity for the rest of her life, charging twenty-five cents to those wishing to see her horribly scarred forehead.[30]

Meanwhile, two keelboats arrived at Prairie du Chien that evening. With them came a harrowing tale of a furious ambush near the mouth of the Bad Axe River, very close to Red Bird's village. The two boats were on a return trip, delivering supplies from Fort Snelling. On the way back, they were called to shore near the Bad Axe and were fired on as soon as they were in range. The first boat, the *Oliver Perry,* got the worst of it. With the boat stuck on a sandbar, the passengers spent much of the afternoon in a tense firefight as Ho-Chunk warriors relentlessly tried to board their vessel. It isn't known whether Red Bird personally directed the attack on the keelboats, though certainly members of his village conducted the attacks— but to a community reeling from the murders at the Gagnier homestead earlier that day, it was irrelevant. The sight of the bullet-ridden keelboat and the bodies of the dead and wounded crew members only added to the general panic. Matters were not helped when it was learned that the dead and wounded crew members were from Prairie du Chien.[31]

Without a local army presence, command fell to the only real federal official left in Prairie du Chien—Indian subagent John Marsh. Agent Nicholas Boilvin had died earlier that year. Marsh decided the best place for local residents to take refuge was in abandoned Fort Crawford, and he sent express messengers to Fort Snelling, St. Louis, and Green Bay, where he knew Territorial Governor Cass was scheduled to arrive for a council with several tribes. In his message to Cass, Marsh appealed for reinforcements and was quick to identify the culprits:

> I am decidedly of the opinion that the body of the [Ho-Chunk] nation are desirous of peace and have no connection with the hostile party—it is believed that the [Ho-chunk] Band of Prairie de la Cross which consists of about One Hundred & Eighty men is alone guilty of the late murders and will not desist till the most severe measures are resorted to, or in fact till they are exterminated.[32]

Little is known of Red Bird's movements after the attacks. The chief and his followers left the Mississippi River and moved toward the Fox and Wisconsin portage area, where several Ho-Chunk villages were located. Lawrence Taliaferro, the Indian agent at Fort Snelling, reported that more than 150 Ho-Chunk had returned to their village above Prairie du Chien to tend to their cornfields. As a protective measure, the Ho-Chunk had occupied most of the river islands in their area. Taliaferro believed they

Lewis Cass, Michigan Territorial Governor and Superintendent of Indian Affairs, in a portrait by Lewis T. Ives after G. P. A. Healy, 1874. WHS MUSEUM OBJECT ID 1942.44

intended to "attack any detachment of troops that may ascend the river and secondly to cut off all persons who may attempt to ascend or descend the Mississippi from this post."[33]

Marsh reported that Red Bird had sent messengers to the Ho-Chunk villages on the Rock River, encouraging others to join in the attacks.[34] Reception to such overtures, however, was cool. Many tribal leaders were not eager to engage in a war against the Great Father. One chief of the Fox River Band even threatened to turn Red Bird in if he came into his area.

As events unfolded along the Mississippi River, Lewis Cass and Thomas McKenney convened their council at Little Lake Butte des Morts. Like Cass, McKenney was an experienced hand at Indian affairs. For years he had served as superintendent of Indian trade for the federal government. In this capacity McKenney oversaw government trading with the numerous tribes along the entire frontier. His department, however, was viewed as a threat by John Jacob Astor, who used his considerable political influence to have the department abolished in 1822. Two years later, McKenney was appointed superintendent of Indian Affairs in Washington, working directly under the secretary of war. Among the entourage accompanying Cass and McKenney at the council was Kinzie, who was temporarily assigned as McKenney's aide.

The council at Butte des Morts included no fewer than ten different tribes and was a continuation of the business started two years before at Prairie du Chien. In addition to continuing discussions of tribal boundary lines, Cass and McKenney hoped to settle a five-year-old intertribal boundary dispute at Green Bay, and a leadership question regarding the Menominee.

Cass learned about the murders along the Mississippi the moment he stepped off the boat at Green Bay. After issuing orders directing the preparation for the council, the governor boarded a canoe and set out down the Fox and Wisconsin Rivers, stopping briefly at Prairie du Chien, and traveling all the way to St. Louis, where he mobilized General Henry Atkinson and 580 soldiers to move north into the heart of Ho-Chunk territory. Cass then returned via Chicago, assessing the situation along the way and rallying local militias against the Ho-Chunk. It was a whirlwind journey that only temporarily delayed the start of the council. Within three weeks, Cass was back at Butte des Morts and plunged himself into negotiations.

The council was held at the foot of an ancient burial mound on the shores of Little Lake Butte des Morts. Cass and McKenney, flanked by two companies of the Second Infantry under the command of Major William Whistler, took turns at the podium addressing the different tribes. Despite the range of issues before the council, the dramatic events involving Red Bird and Prairie du Chien overshadowed the gathering. Early on the

A scene from the council meeting at Butte des Morts, as illustrated by James Otto Lewis, who accompanied Cass and McKenney, ca. 1835. WHI IMAGE ID 3915

two commissioners engaged in a shrewd game of psychological warfare. Throughout the council Cass would address the Ho-Chunk delegation in front of the entire council and read express dispatches from General Atkinson detailing the advance of the US troops into the heart of the Ho-Chunk lands. Cass and McKenney wanted to humiliate the Ho-Chunk and isolate them from their neighboring tribes. They knew that other tribes were watching the situation and might go to war against the Americans if the Ho-Chunk were successful. Continuing their address to the council, the commissioners hammered away at the Ho-Chunk, at one point saying, "We will strike those Winnebagoes so hard they will remember it & their childrens children."[35]

Two days later the commissioners again reported to the council that Atkinson was seeking out the leaders of the attacks and that the general was after Red Bird's son. But in the same breath the commissioners indicated all-out war could yet be averted. "As soon as the Winnebagoes let their people know that the murderers at the Prairie & some of those who attacked the boats must be given up the better. There will be no peace till then."[36]

Throughout the negotiations, the Ho-Chunk were noticeably silent.[37] It must have been extremely unsettling to constantly hear reports of an invading army while one sat in council. Only on August 14, at the end of

the council, did they respond to the commissioner's words. Four Legs rose
and spoke:

> You have always told us to be still, to raise our children, provide for
> our families & not be afraid of your men. But I am afraid of your
> young men at the mines. There are a great many Americans on our
> land, working it without our permission, & I want you to tell our
> Great Father [the President of the United States] to stop it—reach out
> his long arm & draw them back.[38]

The commissioners responded the next day: "We will send to your
father, your request about the people at the Rock River. Your Great Father
will put an end to their encroachments & shall wall around your land so
that none of our people shall go over. We do not intend that our people
shall go on your land."[39] But they quickly followed with a stern warning:

> We are going to open the road from here to that River [Mississippi]
> not with axes but with guns. . . . We have been waiting a great while
> and are tired of it. We will not injure the peaceable. If they surrender
> to us the murderer at Prairie du Chien & three or four of the princi-
> pal men who attacked the keelboats, we will sit still and be satisfied.
> But if they will not, we will not stop but strike until we can get them
> ourselves.[40]

The council adjourned on August 15. Cass returned to Green Bay and
soon departed for Detroit. As a part of the military maneuvers against the
Ho-Chunk, Major William Whistler's two companies, accompanied by
McKenney and Kinzie, moved up the Fox River to establish a camp at the
portage between the Fox and the Wisconsin. There the small command
was to wait for the arrival of General Atkinson and his force.[41]

Whistler and his men had been at the portage for only a day when a
solitary Ho-Chunk warrior approached and announced that Red Bird and
one of his accomplices would surrender the next day. Later in the afternoon, a second Ho-Chunk warrior arrived at the portage and repeated the
same message. The evening brought yet a third messenger. McKenney
interrogated each of the warriors and believed they were sent to Whistler's

encampment to prevent his men from attacking the tribe, which apparently was gathering nearby.[42]

At or around three the following afternoon, September 2, a large crowd of Ho-Chunk approached the encampment on foot and on horseback. Three were carrying flags: two American and one white.[43] As the Indians drew closer to the bank of the Fox River, they began to sing. Those among Whistler's group who were familiar with Indian culture immediately recognized the music as a death song. Some believed Red Bird himself was singing.

As the crowd stopped at the river's edge, a small delegation of Ho-Chunk leaders approached the encampment. Leading the group was Nawkaw Caramaunee, a major chief of the tribe, and with him were Red Bird and his son, Wekaw. Whistler called his command into formation. On his left stood his Indian auxiliary companies of Menominee and New York Indians. On his right flank stood a military band. Red Bird stepped out from the small group of chiefs and stood before Whistler, and all eyes fixed on him.

Kinzie had a front-row view. His past association with the Ho-Chunk and his knowledge of their language made him especially useful to everyone involved. Initially McKenney had directed him to assist Whistler in receiving the prisoners. But when Caramaunee recognized Kinzie, he asked that Kinzie stand beside him and verify that the conversation was interpreted accurately.[44] Two days later Kinzie wrote to a friend about Red Bird:

> He certainly was the best looking Indian in the Nation. He was
> dressed in Sioux [Dakota] dress of white leather has a piece of square
> scarlet cloth over his breast & an ornamental pipe stem with feathers
> & painted green & across his breast. In his left hand was a pipe and in
> his right he held a white flag.[45]

Whistler asked Red Bird and Wekaw to sit down. The band played a somber tune. Listening attentively to the music, Red Bird filled his pipe and smoked. At length a Ho-Chunk chief, perhaps Nawkaw Caramaunee, spoke. He stated that at the Council at Buttes des Morts, the tribe was required to bring in the murderers. They brought in two. The third had run away. The two present had surrendered voluntarily. Twenty horses had been brought along in the hopes that the whites would take them as commutation for the deaths in Prairie du Chien. He asked for leniency for Red Bird and asked that he not be put in chains.[46]

Red Bird listened to all of this. Then he stood up, faced Whistler, and said, "I am ready . . . I do not wish to be put in irons. Let me be free. I have given away my life—it is gone," and here he stooped, took some dust between his finger and thumb, and blew it away, "—I would not take it back. It is gone."[47] If any formal reply was made to Red Bird, it was not recorded. Whistler directed several soldiers to escort Red Bird and Wekaw to a tent and hold them under guard.

General Atkinson and his army arrived at the portage the next day and assumed charge of the prisoners. Atkinson believed more culprits could be rounded up, so he summoned all available Ho-Chunk leaders for another council. Again he demanded that the tribe deliver up those responsible for the murders at Prairie du Chien. Two more warriors were handed over.[48] It is not known just who Atkinson was looking for. He may have been under the assumption that more Ho-Chunk were involved in the Gagnier murders, or he may have been looking for leaders of the keelboat attack. The Ho-Chunk chiefs replied that the others had fled the region but that they would try to bring them in.

Satisfied with the sincerity of the chiefs, Atkinson turned the discussion to matters relating to the trespass of miners on Ho-Chunk land. As Atkinson later reported, "I proceeded to guard the immediate interest of the inhabitants of the Fever river, by entering into written articles with the Winnebagoes, stipulating that the miners should have an unmolested privilege of procuring mineral in the district of country between the Fever river and the Ouisconsin."[49] Atkinson's temporary treaty would be only the beginning of a long series of concessions the Ho-Chunk would now have to make as a result of Red Bird's actions.

For five months after their surrender, Red Bird and his fellow prisoners languished in a guardhouse cell at Fort Crawford. The squalid conditions steadily eroded Red Bird's health, and in February 1828 he succumbed to dysentery. His death cast a shadow over a land already made dreary by a long winter. Though the chief was gone, his fellow prisoners still remained in their cell. This did not sit well with the Ho-Chunk.

In January Joseph Street, the new Indian agent at Prairie du Chien, was inundated by numerous visits from Ho-Chunk leaders. Street shared their views in a letter to Secretary of War James Barbour, including a notable statement from one unidentified Ho-Chunk leader:

> The winter hunting will not last long; the corn moon will come . . .
> When the women are making corn, the young men and warriors will
> be idle, or roaming over the plains; and we fear, when good chiefs
> are away, they will go amongst the whites, get whiskey, and when
> drunk, murder will come. The lead mines and the Winnebagoes are
> too near; white men will carry whiskey where ever they go; Indians
> will buy it when it comes near them—they are maddened by it, and
> murder comes.[50]

5

A Trip to Washington

With the surrender of Red Bird, many settlers believed the Indian scare of the summer was over, and miners again resumed digging for the gray gold. Now they pressed further into Ho-Chunk territory, flouting the terms of Atkinson's treaty. Henry Dodge, leader of the mounted volunteer militia that had accompanied Atkinson up the Wisconsin River the previous summer, began extensive mining operations near present-day Dodgeville. Joseph Street, the new Indian agent at Prairie du Chien, complained to the secretary of war:

> I have sent to the miners engaged in mining on the Winnebago lands, warning them to depart quietly; to which they pay no attention. Gen. H. Dodge, with about one hundred and thirty men, well armed in pistols and rifles, have located themselves twenty or thirty miles within the lines of the Winnebago country, N.E. of Galena, have built a stockade fort, and are raising, smelting, and transporting large quantities of lead.[1]

Dodge had been present at the portage when Atkinson signed his treaty with the Ho-Chunk leaders.[2] He knew the Indians had promised not to harm any miner who trespassed onto their lands. Dodge did not have the authority to enter into Ho-Chunk territory, but his audacity paid off. The lead deposits he discovered were close the surface and easily extracted, and his diggings resulted in one of the largest lodes of lead yet.

Street immediately requested that 180 men from the recently regarrisoned Fort Crawford be sent to remove the miners. To Street's frustration, the garrison was simply too small to offer any help. So the agent was compelled to do nothing. John Connelly, the Indian agent at Galena, was facing similar problems and expressed his frustrations to William Clark at St. Louis: "It is notorious that the spirit of intrusion arose from the encouragement held out by the Supt of the Lead Mines as may easily be proven by the permissions granted to Individuals and promise of protection without any regard to Indian Rights."[3]

Dodge was a noteworthy intruder, but he wasn't the only one. Hundreds of miners were flocking over Ho-Chunk lands, and tribal leaders were powerless to stop them. In their council with General Atkinson the previous summer, the tribe had promised not to harass any miner who set up operations in their territory. The general had promised the Ho-Chunk leaders that commissioners representing the president would come to visit the tribe in the summer of 1828 and settle the matter of the miners. All the chiefs could do was sit and wait—wait for the trial of Red Bird's accomplices to begin, and wait for the commissioners to come. In the meantime, their warriors were growing increasingly angry and were drinking more of the whiskey provided by the white traders.

As the tribe grew more agitated, Governor Cass and other officials considered sending a delegation of Ho-Chunk chiefs to Washington to visit the president that autumn. The journey east would take the leaders through established cities of the United States. The idea was to make an indelible impression on the chiefs, to show them the size and power of their adversary and the hopelessness of their own situation. McKenney supported the idea:

> It would impress upon them opinions of our power which they have
> never had the means of forming; and which it is believed may tend to
> quiet their restlessness, and tame their ferocity. It is most true they
> have never seen, and therefore (having no medium through which
> they could perceive our superiority—) have no conception of their
> own comparative feebleness.[4]

McKenney had been hearing reports that the bulk of the tribe had temporarily concentrated near Lake Winnebago, where they were hunting and stockpiling supplies. He told James Barbour, the US secretary of war, "My opinion is that they mean to strike."[5] McKenney, however, knew of a wife of a notable chief who was urging caution and care among the leaders of the tribe. It was well known that she had traveled east and had "knowledge of our power."[6] McKenney was referring to the wife of Four Legs, who was a Meskwaki and had traveled to New York when she was young. Juliette Kinzie met her several years later and could attest to the reputation of "Madame Four Legs":

> She was a Fox [Meskwaki] woman, and spoke the Chippewa, which is the court language among all the tribes, so that she was often called upon to act as interpreter, and had, in fact, been in the habit of accompanying her husband, and assisting him by her counsels upon all occasions. She was a person of great shrewdness and judgment, and as I afterwards experienced, of strong and tenacious affections.[7]

McKenney was not the only one who believed a show of strength was a good idea. Secretary of War Barbour felt that it was necessary to establish a permanent garrison in the heart of Ho-Chunk territory. Alarmed by the growing discontent of the tribes, Barbour called for the establishment of a new post "for the purpose of watching the movements of the Indians."[8] The newly appointed General of the Army, Alexander Macomb, agreed. Macomb believed the absence of a meaningful American military presence in the region in 1827 had been a major cause of the uprising. This was a departure from the beliefs of his predecessor, Jacob Brown, who had died in February. Brown had believed his policy of concentrating forces at bases like Jefferson Barracks had led to the success in quickly subduing the Ho-Chunk.[9]

Macomb sent out a series of orders that led to a flurry of military activity along the Wisconsin frontier. In addition to regarrisoning Fort Crawford, the army reactivated Fort Dearborn. Macomb also ordered the construction of a new fort at the portage of the Fox and Wisconsin Rivers, where Red Bird had surrendered the summer before. The First Infantry was to build the new post and occupy Prairie du Chien. To impress the Ho-Chunk, the Fifth Regiment, which was stationed at St. Louis, was to move up the Wisconsin and Fox Rivers to Green Bay and the Illinois River to Chicago. Macomb was confident that such a mobilization along the frontier "must have a powerful influence over the Winnebagoes . . . there is every reason to believe that neither the Winnebagoes nor their confederates will attempt any hostilities so long as the troops maintain their present positions."[10]

In July, William Clark told the secretary of war that the unfriendly behavior of the Ho-Chunk was reaching a critical point. Thomas Forsyth, the Indian agent at Rock Island, had reported that members of the tribe had built a fort at Lake Koshkonong (modern-day Fort Atkinson) "to defend themselves against any attacks."[11] Forsyth also reported that whites were mining deep inside Ho-Chunk territory and miners were pilfering supplies such as corn from Ho-Chunk settlements.[12] Added to this was a letter from John Connelly, the agent at Fever River, who reported, "There is every probability of an Indian fuss. The miners are determined to take the Kosh-Ke-bone [Koshkonong] village mines . . . by force."[13] The Ho-Chunk, reported Connelly, were shooting "horses, oxen, and kick some of the intruders, when they find them in small numbers."[14]

Kinzie's whereabouts after the surrender of Red Bird are unknown, though it is presumed he returned to Detroit and resumed his duties as private secretary to Cass. In the middle of August 1828, though, he was back in Green Bay with his boss. This time the two men were joined by Pierre Menard, the Indian agent at Peoria, Illinois, to hold a council with the Ho-Chunk, Ojibwe, Potawatomi, and Sauk and Meskwaki. Four tribes attended, but the council was primarily held for the Ho-Chunk, and the entire negotiations focused on obtaining land cessions of the lead region.

Though Cass attempted to use a conciliatory tone, his negotiations got nowhere. A Ho-Chunk chief of the Rock River Band named Kaxiskaga, or White Crow, rose to reply to Cass. White Crow was a rough-looking man, about forty-five years old, tall and slim, with a hawk nose. He wore a black handkerchief over one eye, which had been seriously damaged years earlier in a fight. Addressing the governor's land cession proposal, White Crow slyly stated, "We cannot give you an answer now, because there are not enough of us here. Next spring we will answer you one way or the other. After we have consulted the whole nation you shall hear it."[15]

It was a tactic to buy time. The Ho-Chunk had not come to the council to sell land. They had hoped to keep the miners at bay.

Finally, the group reached a compromise of sorts and signed a new treaty on August 25, 1828. Cass and the other commissioners acknowledged there weren't enough Ho-Chunk members present to agree to sell any lands. Still, the commissioners drew a provisional boundary line that ran from the mouth of the Wisconsin River to Blue Mounds, then southeast to the Rock River (near what today is Rockford, Illinois), and finally down the Rock River to the Mississippi—in essence, carving out the entire region known to hold lead deposits.[16] According to the new treaty, the US government could occupy lands within the provisional boundary. This was not to say the lands were open for settlers or miners. It would still be necessary to gain permission from the federal government before whites could enter the region.

But Cass was adamant. If any miner legally or illegally crossed over into Ho-Chunk land, the tribe was not to hurt him in any way. If problems arose, the tribe could appeal to the president for help.[17] The agreement was to be only temporary until a council could be held, presumably in 1829, when the lands within the provisional boundary would be ceded to the United States. Any compensation the tribes could expect for damages done by miners in the past, or the future, would be made when the Ho-Chunk sold their land.

It was a rough deal. One could suppose that no one came away from it totally satisfied. Cass and Menard had hoped to buy the entire lead region but got permission only to use the land. The Ho-Chunk had hoped to keep the miners off their land but had to settle for postponing land cessions for a year. At least there was finally a boundary line that defined the lead region. From a legal standpoint the issue of trespassing miners was finally resolved.

—◁II▷—

In September the army made good on its plans to establish Fort Winnebago, a permanent garrison in the heart of Ho-Chunk territory. In late August, Major David Twiggs, of the First US Infantry, received orders from General Macomb directing him to proceed to the portage with three companies to establish a military post.[18] On September 7, Twiggs reported his arrival:

> I have selected a position for the fort on the right bank of the Fox
> river, immediately opposite the portage. The Indians, I am told, are

very much dissatisfied with the location of troops here; as yet I have
not been able to see any of the chiefs, consequently cannot say with
any certainty what their dispositions are.[19]

Coincidentally, Twiggs had selected the very spot where Red Bird had
surrendered almost exactly a year earlier. The new fort was unimposing. It
consisted of six buildings, including barracks, officers' quarters, and store-
houses, arranged around a square. A tight budget meant there was no pali-
sade or wall to protect the garrison.[20] Two blockhouses, situated on opposite
corners of the square, offered the only real defense in the event of an attack.

In early October, as Fort Winnebago was nearing completion, a delegation of Ho-Chunk leaders gathered to travel east to see their "Great Father,"
the president of the United States. Many in the delegation were anxious to
go. In contrast to McKenney and Cass, who felt such a trip would overawe
the leaders with the power and superiority of the United States, the chiefs
were concerned about the prolonged confinement of their warriors at Fort
Crawford, and they were eager to talk with the Great Father and complain
in person about the trespassing miners. Perhaps he could do something
the Americans in Michigan Territory could not.

Both Cass and McKenney agreed that Kinzie was just the man to lead
the delegation on their journey. Sixteen members of the tribe were selected to make the trip. Pierre Paquette, a fur trader from the portage who
was fluent in both Ho-Chunk and French, served as an interpreter. Cass
also sent along his personal secretary, and Kinzie's cousin, Robert Allen
Forsyth. It was a reunion for the two men, who had both come a long way
since their days as teacher and student in Chicago. Forsyth had attended
West Point and had accompanied Cass on a journey throughout the Michigan Territory in 1820.[21]

Joining them on the trip were representatives of two of the most in-
fluential families in the Ho-Chunk Nation, the Caramaunee and Decorah.
Recently a feud had broken out between the two powerful factions, who
were rivals for tribal leadership. They both had insisted on sending representatives with the delegation to keep an eye on each other. Among the
delegation was Nawkaw Caramaunee, considered the principal chief of the
Nation. Nawkaw, said to be ninety-four years old, had been a prominent

leader in the tribe for decades. He had been with Tecumseh when he was killed at the Battle of the Thames and had been with Red Bird at his surrender. White War Eagle, the head of the Decorah family, went along, as did Dandy, who came from the village at the head of Lake Winnebago. White Crow, the spirited orator at the recent council at Green Bay, represented the Rock River Band.[22]

The initial leg of the trip took the group to Detroit via the steamboat *Henry Clay.* The size of the territorial capital did not seem to impress the chiefs. At least one of the delegation commented that the Ho-Chunk Nation was "not only more brave and virtuous than the whites, but equal in number to them."[23] From Detroit they sailed by steamer across Lake Erie to Buffalo. The overland route took them from Buffalo to Utica to Schenectady to Albany. Interestingly, though the route took them near the Erie Canal, there is no mention in the expense or newspaper accounts of the delegation using the waterway. From Albany they traveled down the Hudson to New York City.[24]

In New York, Kinzie and Forsyth took the chiefs to Washington Square to view a specially organized parade and inspection of the city militia led by General Jacob Morton, the senior militia officer of the city. An account published in the *Connecticut Journal* noted, "They appeared to be gratified, especially with the horsemen. An arrangement was made to have the cannon discharged at the moment the Indians were passing them in the rear, without their being appraised of their intention, to see what effect it would produce; and strange as it may seem, they did not move a muscle or appear to regard it."[25] At the end of the parade the chiefs were presented to the mayor and "other officers of the city government."

The great city, it seemed, was quite taken by the delegation. The Ho-Chunk leaders were the first of their Nation ever to visit the city, and many New Yorkers were amazed at their dress and customs. Businessmen tried to increase their profits by sending the chiefs complimentary tickets to various shows, in hopes that their presence would draw in larger audiences. The delegation remained in the city for a week. Kinzie and Forsyth accompanied the chiefs to the city arsenal, the navy yard, fortifications, Peale's Museum, and the Battery, where they were among a crowd of thirty thousand spectators to witness the flight of a hot air balloon.

Still, the chiefs refused to openly comment on the scenes they witnessed. When asked about their impressions of the United States and of New York, they scoffed and commented on the foolishness of Americans. When pressed for his thoughts on the balloon, Nawkaw replied, "Think! Think nothing of it."[26]

Leaving New York, the chiefs traveled through Philadelphia, where they stopped long enough to view a performance of the French Opera. Their presence at the theater caused quite a stir, as a reporter for the Philadelphia *National Gazette* reported:

> The "sons of the forest" were painted and accoutered in character, and raised with one voice their shrill note of salutation in answer to the first acclamations of the spectators. They arrived about the middle of the first piece, nearly filled one of the stage-boxes.[27]

The chiefs were escorted to the middle of the theater, where they could have a better view and possibly to make further impression on the audience. As the local newspaper later reported:

> They continued to attract much attention, but left the house before the end of the performance. The large number of ladies in the first row of boxes seemed to feel particular interest and some alarm, at this sudden and strange apparition; we observed that the Winnebagoes gazed around on the beautiful array, with more apparent emotion of curiosity and pleasure than is usual with the Indian race on such occasions.[28]

On October 31, the group finally arrived in Washington and settled into Tennison's Hotel, near the offices of the War Department. Washington, however, would prove to be less welcoming than New York or Philadelphia. Indian delegations were common in the capital city, and problems arose whenever liquor was on hand. The leaders would fight among themselves or confront passersby in front of the hotel. Ruffians would wait outside the hotel and pounce upon the unsuspecting chiefs, sometimes beating them severely.[29]

The delegation remained in Washington for six weeks. As they waited for the chance to meet with the president, the leaders were taken to special exhibitions and were serenaded by local bands. In late November, the chiefs added to the festivities by staging a war dance for the general entertainment of the citizens.[30]

The leaders of the Ho-Chunk Nation finally met with President John Quincy Adams on November 29, 1828. The visit took place in the White House, possibly in the recently decorated East Room. A witness to the meeting later noted in the Washington National Intelligencer "the ornamental hanging, the carpeting, the mirrors, the tables of marble slab, the central chandelier with this sparkling lustres, the sofas, and mahogany chairs, with seats of crimson damask. All are perceived to comport with good taste, and yet not to offend the strict maxims of judicious simplicity."[31] The room also contained a large fireplace, a "blazing council-fire" above which hung a full-length portrait of George Washington.

According to newspaper accounts, the delegation was led by an "interpreter," who was most likely Pierre Paquette.[32] President Adams greeted the leaders individually as each entered. With the president stood the secretary of war, representatives of Congress, Lewis Cass, and numerous onlookers. After everyone was seated, the president served Madeira and macaroons.[33] For a moment everyone enjoyed the refreshments. Then Nawkaw Caramaunee stood up and began the dialogue. Stepping forward with a long-stemmed pipe in his hands, he faced the president and said:

> Father, I am glad to see you. I hold out this pipe, and I take your hand in friendship. Father, a cloud has been between us. It was thick and black, I thought once it would never be removed. But now I see your face. It looks upon me pleasantly.[34]

It took a moment for Adams to comprehend what the chief had said. Nawkaw spoke in Ho-Chunk, which was translated into French by Paquette, the interpreter who had accompanied the chiefs, and then turned into English by a second interpreter.[35]

The pipe was lit and passed to everyone in the room—first to the president, then to his entourage, and then the chiefs. When it came back to

Nawkaw, he gave it to the president and asked that he keep it. In accepting
the pipe, Adams turned to the interpreters and replied:

> Say to this Chief, I rejoice to see him. He and his brethren are wel-
> come to me as my children. Tell him, it has grieved me that a cloud
> has been between us; but I am pleased equally with him, that it has
> been dissipated.[36]

The president went on to say that if he ever heard that the Ho-Chunk
had made war against the United States, he would not believe it, for he
had the word of the Ho-Chunk, which was, in addition to the pipe, a true
token of their sincerity.

When Nawkaw and Adams had finished their exchange, another chief
rose to address the president. He asked for clemency for the warriors who
remained confined at Fort Crawford. Apparently Adams was prepared for
this request. To the pleasure of the Ho-Chunk delegation, he granted it.[37]
Within moments the president signed the pardon, but there was a catch.
Adams asked the chiefs to sell their lands in the lead region. The lands
had been the source of the trouble between the two peoples, the president
said. He argued that the land was no longer of any real use to the tribe. He
assured that a fair price would be paid, and that the sale would establish a
lasting friendship between the two peoples.[38]

The chiefs were taken aback. For a time they talked among themselves.
Finally Nawkaw rose and replied to Adams that they did not have the power
to sell any tribal lands. The matter had to be taken back and considered by
the entire tribe. Because the Great Father had been so good as to pardon
the two warriors at Fort Crawford, they agreed to take the request to their
people. Nawkaw concluded with a plea:

> Father, if you send commissioners to treat with us, let them be good
> men; if agents to dwell among us, let them be honest men. And do
> not try to convert us to the habits of your children, or to make us like
> the Indians of Green Bay. We wish to live as we have lived, and to fol-
> low, and to abide by, the customs of our fore-fathers.[39]

Nawkaw's speech ended the negotiations. After another round of refreshments and another smoking of the pipe, the leaders left the president and began their journey home.

Finally, Kinzie was back at Detroit, but soon he was preparing for a new job. As the army built the new Fort Winnebago at the portage, Cass was making plans for a new Indian agency to be located adjacent to the fort, to help keep a watchful eye over the troublesome tribe. This was not to be a full agency. There were budget limitations, and full agencies already stood nearby at Green Bay and Prairie du Chien.

The subagency needed an agent. And Cass had just the man for the job—a young man fluent in multiple Native languages, the son of a prominent fur trader, a former employee of the powerful American Fur Company, and his own private secretary. On December 29, 1828, John Harris Kinzie was appointed as Indian subagent for the newly established Indian subagency at Fort Winnebago.

6

THE TREATY OF 1829

John H. Kinzie was twenty-five years old when he was appointed Indian subagent in December 1828. Many agents were in their forties when first taking the post; but even though Kinzie was younger, his upbringing on the Great Lakes frontier and his mastery of multiple Native languages made him more qualified than many of his counterparts. Some, like Lawrence Taliaferro, the agent at St. Peters (modern-day Minneapolis–St. Paul), were former army officers. Others were newspaper editors. Many were appointed because of family or political connections. George Boyd, agent at Mackinaw and later Green Bay, was a brother-in-law to President John Quincy Adams.

Agents coming from the fur trade were perhaps best prepared for the job. Though often at odds with the federal laws, fur traders were familiar with the Indian service and were more likely to be familiar with Native American culture and traditions. Regardless of their backgrounds, the one commonality among the men appointed as Indian agents was that everyone learned on the job.

Kinzie's appointment was both operationally pragmatic and politically calculated. Kinzie knew Cass personally and was related to several other agents already in the region. Alexander Wolcott, the agent at Chicago, was a brother-in-law—and Wolcott was Juliette Kinzie's uncle, which also made him John Kinzie's uncle-in-law. Thomas Forsyth, agent at Rock Island, was an uncle. And Kinzie's previous employment with the American Fur Company was yet another asset.

The Fort Winnebago subagency was an anomaly in the Indian field service and serves as a good illustration of the inconsistent nature of the

Young John Kinzie, ca. 1830. CHICAGO HISTORY MUSEUM, ICHI-39627

federal Indian policy. As Lewis Cass noted in his report to Congress in 1829, the government from time to time established an "extra" agency. John Kinzie was considered an extra subagent and was placed in charge of "Winnebagoes and Menominees frequenting the Portage of the Ouis-consin."[1] Subagents were usually subordinate to a full agent. The principal agency for the Ho-Chunk was at Prairie du Chien, and the agent there, Joseph Street, reported not to Cass but to William Clark, who presided from St. Louis. In 1831, when a second subagency for the Ho-Chunk was established along the Rock River, the agent there, Henry Gratiot, operated independently but, like Street, reported to William Clark. There was also a full agent for the Menominee at Green Bay, Henry Brevoort, who could technically be seen as Kinzie's superior.

The portage was a dividing point when it came to federal administration of army posts as well as Indian agencies. West of the portage, agents reported to William Clark in St. Louis. East of the portage, agents, including Kinzie, reported to Lewis Cass in Detroit. But where Kinzie really stood out was with regard to his independent status. He reported neither to Street nor to Brevoort, a unique status that would be a source of friction between Kinzie and his peers in the years to come. Street never accepted the independence of the Fort Winnebago subagency. The close relationship between Kinzie and Cass also attracted the ire of Samuel Stambaugh, who succeeded Brevoort at Green Bay in 1830 and complained directly to the secretary of war:

> *Mr. Jno. H. Kinzie* was appointed Sub Agent within this agency in 1828 to reside at Fort Winnebago about 120 miles from this place, at the portage of the Ouisconsin river. He received his pay from Maj. Brevoort it appears, *one year* but by some process he was last year made *independent of the agent here,* and is now accountable to no power but Govr. Cass—Yet I am called upon to *issue licenses to traders* at that place, and, am made responsible for trespass committed![2]

Winter weather and lack of roads prevented Kinzie from arriving at Fort Winnebago until June 17. Though Indian agencies often were located near army installations, they were separate entities. Once Kinzie arrived at the fort, he found that the army had granted him a few surplus log buildings, but otherwise Kinzie had to build his agency from scratch. He did not even have a blacksmith—an essential component for any agency providing free services to local Indians, including, among other things, repairs for firearms. Nor did he have an interpreter, which for the most part was not a problem, thanks to Kinzie's language skills, although he was not able to speak Menominee. Serving as his own interpreter provided an additional $480 beyond the annual $500 salary he received as subagent.[3]

Upon his arrival at Fort Winnebago, Kinzie found a letter waiting for him from Pierre Menard, Indian agent at Peoria, directing him to bring the Indians in his area to Prairie du Chien for a large council. The dramatic

Juliette Kinzie's drawing of Fort Winnebago that was used to illustrate *Wau-Bun*. WHI
IMAGE ID 6125

events of the previous two years had laid the foundation for the first major
land cession of the Ho-Chunk Nation. That spring President Jackson had appointed Menard and Colonel John McNiel to purchase the entire lead region.
Menard had been with Cass the previous summer, at the council at Green
Bay, and was therefore personally acquainted with efforts to acquire the
mining district. McNiel, colonel of the First Infantry, was a battle-hardened
veteran of the War of 1812 but was not experienced in Indian affairs.[4]

Menard and McNiel were charged with the difficult task of purchasing
all the lead-bearing lands east of the Mississippi and south of the Wisconsin River. In essence they were to arrange for the purchase of nearly
all of southern Wisconsin and northern Illinois. It would require them to
create treaties with not only the Ho-Chunk, but also a confederation of
Potawatomi, Ottawa, and Ojibwe, collectively referred to at the time as
the Illinois tribes.[5]

Kinzie was doubtful that the two men could succeed. He wrote to Cass,
"The commissioners will no doubt, have a great deal of trouble to effect the
purchase of the mining district. Almost every inhabitant in the country
has a claim of some kind and pretty heavy ones too."[6]

Kinzie was among those asking for a special appropriation. He needed
funds to erect a blacksmith at his agency. Blacksmiths provided free metal-

working services to local Indians and were a powerful incentive to draw tribesmen to the agency. Kinzie could apply for an appropriation from Congress, but that would take time and, given the excessively stringent nature of the Jackson administration, was not guaranteed.

Many of the Ho-Chunk were disinclined to go to the council. They had good reason, as they knew major land cessions were coming. Major Twiggs, the commander of Fort Winnebago, had been urging local chiefs to attend, but he wasn't having much luck. Only with Kinzie's help was Twiggs able to assemble and send a delegation of Ho-Chunk to Prairie du Chien.

Kinzie's prediction that Menard and McNiel's council would fail wasn't far off the mark. But the first problem lay not with potential claimants, but with the two commissioners themselves.

Menard and McNiel had met in St. Louis that April to discuss their assignment. They apparently had such a serious disagreement over how to conduct their business that they separated without making any decisions whatsoever. As far as anyone knew, the two men had then refused to correspond with each other. Even such a simple matter as the appointment of a staff secretary was left unattended. After forty-nine days with no action, President Jackson personally intervened and appointed a third commissioner, Caleb Atwater, to get the council back on track.[7]

If that was not enough, Atwater learned from William Clark that no money had been appropriated to transport the commissioners to Prairie du Chien, let alone buy the necessary presents and provisions for a large council.[8] Jackson wanted the lead region and gave considerable latitude to the commissioners to achieve this goal, but for the time being, there was no money from the government to pay for any part of the treaty process. The entire project would have to be paid in advance by the commissioners themselves. In his instructions, Secretary of War John Eaton stressed that the president urged "ultimate economy." It was a clear message: get the lead region; it is important to the security of the nation and, by the way, do not spend too much money doing it.[9]

When the commissioners finally arrived in July, they were met by no fewer than fifteen hundred Indians. Among the throng of tribes and government officials, the commissioners were greeted by Kinzie, who had arrived with his delegation. Throughout the following weeks, Kinzie would serve as commissary, dispensing supplies to the attendees.

After several days of preparations, the great council began on July 20. It must have been quite a spectacle. As Atwater remembered, "The commissioners sat on a raised bench, facing the Indian chiefs; on each side of them stood the officers of the army in full dresses, while the solders, in their best attire, appeared in bright array, on the sides of the council shade."[10] The council attracted a lot of attention and drew an audience from "persons . . . not only from *every large city in this union* [Atwater's emphasis] but even from Paris & London & Liverpool!"[11]

From the start, though, there was a problem with language. As Atwood later recalled, "The Indians of all the tribes and nations on the treaty ground attended, and requested to have translated to them, severally, what we said to each tribe."[12] This was not an easy task, for there were representatives from Ho-Chunk, Ojibwe, Sauk and Meskwaki, Ottawa, Potawatomi, Dakota, and Menominee—a total of eight different tribes at the council.

The commissioners opened the council with a speech professing peaceful intentions and assuring the chiefs that they came as friends. But they wasted no time in getting to the matter at hand. "Brothers and Friends. . . . ," they began, "Your Great Father wishes to avoid all the difficulties that might hereafter arise between his white and red children,

The council meeting at Fond du Lac in 1826; this scene would have been very similar to any of the six treaty councils Kinzie attended. WHI IMAGE ID 95720

and for this reason alone, he wishes to buy all the land you claim East and South of the Wisconsin River."

They were willing to pay "the full value of the land you may sell him, and more than you can make by hunting the small game that may remain on it."[13] Recalling the agreement made at Green Bay the year before, the commissioners reminded the tribes that "you have promised to sell what you claim on the Mississippi and he [the president] depends on your promise."[14] (Unfortunately, the council journal states only that the "commissioners" spoke and does not specify which commissioner was speaking.)

The chiefs, however, remembered the negotiations of the previous year. They demanded the annuity payment promised to them by Cass and Menard. The Potawatomi, in particular, refused to consider selling their lands until they received their payment. But the Mississippi River was unusually low that summer, delaying the arrival of a steamer that carried the goods the three men had planned to use as payment for the treaty. The commissioners were in a bind.

In that moment, it appeared the negotiations might break down completely. At this critical juncture, Pierre Menard fell ill and remained on his sickbed at Street's house for several days. At nearly the same time, Colonel McNiel also fell ill and withdrew to the confines of Fort Crawford. This left only Caleb Atwater to continue the negotiations. Chief Nawkaw Caramaunee warned Atwater that the Ho-Chunk were steadily growing restless; many were threatening to attack the commissioners should they stray too far from the protection of the fort. The venerable chief advised Atwater to take refuge within the garrison.[15]

Amid this contentious atmosphere, Keokuk, a leader of the Sauk and Meskwaki, arrived with almost two hundred warriors. Atwater pulled Keokuk aside and asked for assistance. Keokuk obliged by ordering his warriors, in full view of the Ho-Chunk, to commence a war dance. At the same time someone spread the rumor that thirty steamboats full of American soldiers were moving up the Mississippi River.[16]

Not long after the arrival of Keokuk's warriors, the boat carrying the provisions for the council finally arrived. Almost immediately, and quite conveniently, the health of McNiel and Menard was restored and the council resumed.[17]

The Illinois tribes agreed to sell all their lands on the east bank of the

Mississippi, as well as a tract of land just north of Chicago. In exchange, the tribes would receive a permanent annual annuity of sixteen thousand dollars. In addition they would receive twelve thousand dollars' worth of trade goods by October, a blacksmith, hunting rights to the ceded lands as long as the federal government owned the property, and the elimination of back debts owed to a number of creditors. On July 29, the Illinois tribes signed the treaty. Half of the commissioners' work was done. Kinzie and his family also benefited from this agreement when the Potawatomi allocated thirty-five hundred dollars for his family for damages incurred by the tribe during the War of 1812.

But difficulties remained with the Ho-Chunk. At first, the tribe was not fully aware of the amount of land the Americans expected them to cede. When they found out, they were dismayed. One leader commented, "We did not wish to sell you so large a piece, but we were requested to let a little more go."[18] Hoo-Wan-ne-ka, or Little Elk, a chief from the portage area, rose and suggested an alternate boundary proposal. The commissioners found this unacceptable and replied, "We have seen the line you show us— but we want more; we believe it would be in your interest to give to Duck Creek [just south of present day Portage], and thence straight to the Four Lakes [Madison] that the boundary line will be like a wall between us."[19]

The negotiations went back and forth. The council negotiations were tedious and complex. The commissioners would meet with the Illinois tribes one day and the Ho-Chunk the next. Sessions were held in the morning and again in the afternoon. If language barriers were not enough of a problem, convincing the tribes to sell massive tracts of land was. Further complicating matters were numerous local traders and residents who were harassing the commissioners with individual requests for land cessions or payment of debts from the different tribes. The Ho-Chunk chiefs wanted to grant parcels of land to Charles Gratiot and John Kinzie—possibly their way of providing some means for a blacksmith. Colonel David Twiggs requested lumber for Fort Winnebago.[20] The negotiations tried the patience of every participant and drove at least one chief to complain that his own leaders were dragging their feet.[21]

Reminded of their meeting with the president and their promise to sell their lead-bearing lands, the Ho-Chunk finally gave in and agreed to a new boundary. Little Elk, in exasperation, cried out, "Where in the name of God shall we and our families live if we give more . . . We and our Chiefs agreed to give more and thought we were parting with a large tract—although *I suppose* you think it small."[22]

At noon on July 31, Menard, McNiel, and Atwater met with the Ho-Chunk and presented the formal terms of sale. The Ho-Chunk were to sell all of their lands east of the Mississippi River, south of the Wisconsin River, north of the Rock River, and west of the Pecatonica River. This amounted to 2.9 million acres of land. In return, the tribe would receive a cash annuity of eighteen thousand dollars for thirty years, an immediate payment of thirty thousand dollars in trade goods, plus annual payments of three thousand pounds of tobacco and fifty barrels of salt for thirty years. In addition, the tribe was to receive the services of three blacksmiths to operate at Prairie du Chien, Fort Winnebago, and an undesignated point along the Rock River.[23] At the very end of the proposal, and among the last stipulations laid out in the treaty, was a special allotment of two sections of land for Therese Gagnier and her two children, Francois and Louise. Therese Gagnier was also to receive fifty dollars every year for fifteen years. The money was to come out of the annual annuity of the Ho-Chunk.

On August 1, in open council, the chiefs of the Ho-Chunk Nation signed the treaty. Reflecting on what must have been a long and very tense experience, Joseph Street wrote in triumphant jubilation to Lawrence Taliaferro, "The long agony is past!—The Winnebago Treaty is over, and the whole mining district is ours."[24]

It's doubtful the chiefs of the Ho-Chunk Nation looked upon the Treaty of 1829 in such laudatory terms. This was the Ho-Chunk's first significant land cession in its history. It was a direct result of the "Winnebago War" of 1827. The murders at the Gagnier homestead and the subsequent keelboat attacks had carried the Ho-Chunk Nation from independence to a near total submission to US authority and significant loss of land. For the Ho-Chunk, the next eight years would bring increasing hardship and, eventually, outright removal from the land that was to become Wisconsin.

Kinzie was simply glad the affair was over. In writing to Cass, he said, "I shall leave for Fort Winnebago tomorrow or the next day, and shall be glad to get away from such a set as has come from St. Louis."[25]

7

INDIAN AGENT AT THE PORTAGE

Kinzie returned with his delegation back to Fort Winnebago but did not remain there long. Within a few weeks he was on the road again, accompanying his brother-in-law, Alexander Wolcott, on a trip east to visit family. The trip was the first of many personal journeys Kinzie would make during his tenure as subagent, leading Samuel Stambaugh, the Indian agent at Green Bay, to bitterly complain that Kinzie did not seem "to be employed more than *one month out of the year* [Stambaugh's emphasis]."[1] This trip in particular had an important consequence: Kinzie would meet Wolcott's niece, Juliette Augusta Magill.

Juliette had been aware of Kinzie for some time; Wolcott's letters home relayed stories of the Illinois frontier and often mentioned a young man from Chicago. Wolcott had known Kinzie since at least 1823, when he'd married Kinzie's sister Ellen.

Kinzie and Juliette met in her grandparents' home in Boston. To Juliette, John's frontier background represented an irresistible romantic image, and the two quickly fell in love.

Juliette, a native of Middletown, Connecticut, was three years younger than John, educated, with an artistic bent. Her first schooling took place at a boarding school in New Haven, Connecticut, where she also received private lessons in Latin and "modern languages" from her Uncle Wolcott, who at the time was studying at nearby Yale.[2] Juliette later attended the recently established Troy Female Seminary (still in existence today as the Emma Willard School) in Troy, New York, the first school in the country to offer higher education for women. Unfortunately Juliette's father's financial reverses required that she return to her family, who by then had

Juliette Kinzie with her daughter Nellie, 1838. REPRINTED WITH PERMISSION FROM GIRL
SCOUTS OF THE USA

moved to Fishkill, New York. She spent the next few years immersed in
painting, writing, learning the piano, and tutoring her younger brothers. [3]

Though Juliette was well versed in music and painting, writing was
her passion. Over the course of her life Juliette would write three novels;
a pamphlet on the 1812 Battle at Fort Dearborn; and a popular memoir,
Wau-Bun, that described her life on the Wisconsin frontier. She had a
knack for descriptive narrative, as is evidenced in *Wau-Bun*, and she often
revealed a self-deprecating sense of humor and an adventurous spirit. For

example, on a return trip from Chicago to Fort Winnebago in the spring of 1831, Juliette had prepared a special cover for her fellow female traveling companions to protect them from the weather:

> To guard against the burning effect of the sun and the prairie winds upon our faces, I had, during some of the last days of my visit, prepared for each of us a mask of brown linen, with the eyes, nose, and mouth fitted to accommodate our features; and to enhance the hideousness of each, I had worked eye-brows, lashes, and a circle around the opening for the mouth in black silk. Gathered in plaits under the chin, and with strings to confine them above and below, they furnished a complete protection against the sun and wind, though nothing can be imagined more frightful than the appearance we presented when fully equipped. It was who should be called the ugliest.[4]

The visual effects were telling when, during a rest stop, the three women entered a dwelling where several Indians sat on the floor smoking:

> They raised their eyes as we appeared, and never shall I forget the expression of wonder and horror depicted on the countenances of both. Their lips relaxed until the pipe of one fell upon the floor. Their eyes seemed starting from their heads, and raising their outspread hands, as if to wave us from them, they slowly ejaculated, "Manitou" (a spirit).[5]

John and Juliette were married in August 1830 and were soon on their way back to Fort Winnebago.[6] On the return trip the newlyweds stopped off at Detroit, where Kinzie picked up the first annuity payments from the Treaty of 1829.

Arriving at Fort Winnebago, the young couple was warmly greeted by Twiggs and his wife, Elizabeth, who was particularly excited to meet Juliette. Elizabeth had been the only white woman at the fort and was desperate to have a female companion. At the insistence of the Twiggses, the Kinzies set up house inside the fort. A young lieutenant, Jefferson Davis, quartermaster for the post and future president of the Confederate States of America, graciously gave up his quarters to the newlyweds.[7]

That fall Kinzie sent messengers south to the Ho-Chunk villages along the Rock River and north to Lake Winnebago, notifying the Indians of his agency to come to the portage to receive their payment. Kinzie's role in distributing the annuity payments inspired the Potawatomi, and later the Ho-Chunk, to call him "Shaw-nee-au-kee," or "the silver man," a nickname the Potawatomi had also once bestowed upon Kinzie's father.[8]

The agency became a lively place during annuity payments. As Juliette later remembered, "The woods were now brilliant with the many tints of autumn, and the scene around was further enlivened by groups of Indians, in all directions, and their lodges, which were scattered here and there, in the vicinity of the Agency buildings."[9] Numerous traders were there as well, ready to sell their goods to a people now flush with silver coins.

Various presents and fifteen thousand dollars' worth of silver had to be distributed to several thousand Ho-Chunks. It was a careful process. The heads of the different lodges, or residential structures that could accommodate eighty to one hundred people, had to be registered, and they in turn had to report the number of individuals in their lodge. The tally usually was made in the form of sticks, one for each person. It was too big a job for one man, so officers from the fort helped count out and deliver the payment.

The process didn't end there. With each annuity payment came inevitable claims made upon the Ho-Chunk from a variety of fur traders and other businessmen. If Kinzie believed a claim was justified, he made the payment. If, however, a claim was questionable, he gathered what documentation was available and sent the matter to the territorial governor and superintendent of Indian affairs in Detroit, who reviewed the claims and sent them to Washington for approval by the president.

It was a procedure that could take months, if not years, before any settlement was achieved.[10] One claimant, Henry Perdruville, choose to sidestep the process and in the spring of 1832 wrote directly to Elbert Herring, the commissioner of Indian affairs in Washington, complaining that his claim of $140 for "depredations" committed by several Ho-Chunk two years before was never paid. The nature of the depredations was never recorded, though most likely it was damage to livestock or physical property. Kinzie wrote Herring, noting that Perdruville had never filed a claim with him. If he had received such a claim, "I should certainly have placed it before

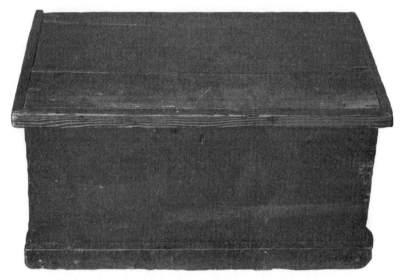

Kinzie likely kept the silver for the annuity payments in this box, now in the collections of the Indian Agency House in Portage. COURTESY OF THE AUTHOR

the Indian chiefs, for their approval or disapproval, and would have sent it with the other claims to Gov. Cass, to be forwarded to the President for this decision."[11]

Successfully making the annuity payments sometimes required that Kinzie guard the process from other agents—as when Henry Gratiot, the subagent at Rock River, tried to divert Kinzie's annual payments to his own subagency instead. Gratiot was deeply involved in several business interests in addition to his duties as a subagent. Some of his associates were linked to the fur trade and were not above using alcohol in their business dealings. Kinzie feared that shifting annuity payments to the Rock River subagency was simply a ploy to allow Gratiot's business associates easier access to the Ho-Chunk and their annuity funds.

Gratiot was well mannered and affable and was deeply involved in both lead mining operations and the fur trade. He was born in St. Louis, the son of a notable French fur trader in the Great Lakes and Upper Mississippi Valley regions. In 1825 with his brother John, Gratiot moved his family into the newly opened lead region of Illinois. After running smelting operations north of Dixon's Ferry, he moved his family to the Galena area and engaged in mining and smelting operations.

Around 1827, Gratiot negotiated an independent agreement with the Rock River Ho-Chunk for the right to mine in their territory. The brothers settled near modern-day Schullsburg and began extensive smelting operations near a "magnificent grove of timber" soon known as Gratiot's Grove. By 1829, Gratiot's Grove had grown into an active community with a post office, busy smelting operations, and a dry goods store.

Henry Gratiot. WHI IMAGE ID 91186

Gratiot was known as being able to both relate to and, in some cases, control the Indians in his vicinity. Gratiot attended the treaty of Green Bay in 1828 and the council the following year at Prairie du Chien. He lobbied for years to become a subagent for the Rock River Ho-Chunk—a post that was finally granted in 1831. The position allowed him to straddle both private business interests and governmental roles. But for Kinzie, Gratiot was a rival not to be trusted—a man who, as Kinzie complained in a letter to Cass, "avails himself of every occasion to prejudice the Indians, as much as in his power against this agency."[12]

Gratiot wasn't the only colleague who caused Kinzie trouble. Kinzie's independent status rankled Joseph Street, who considered himself the senior agent to the Ho-Chunk. One historian described Street as a "pompous, garrulous" man. Writing to Secretary of War John Eaton, Street took full credit for the success of the land cessions gained at the Treaty of 1829. "It will be seen, that I have uniformly assured the Government of the friendly disposition of these Indians, that I had sounded them on the subject of the sale of their lead lands, and that they were disposed to sell."[13]

Street, a native of Virginia, immigrated to Kentucky in 1806, where he purchased the newspaper *Western World*. Street wasted no time in using the newspaper as a platform for attacking former vice president Aaron Burr and several of Burr's associates. Burr, at the time, was involved in a clandestine plot to seize land from the Spanish, who still controlled lands west of the Mississippi, including Texas, and establish his own country. Burr was already a controversial figure—he was a powerful politician in New

York and a former vice president of the United States, and he had killed Alexander Hamilton, the first treasurer of the United States, in a duel.

Burr was traveling through Kentucky seeking support for his scheme, despite attempts to keep it a secret. During a stopover at Frankfurt, Kentucky, a ball was organized in Burr's honor. Many of the region's social and political elite were invited, including Street. Burr's associates thought they might use the occasion to gain revenge against Street for slandering their reputations. They assaulted Street as he entered the ball, though Street fought back. He was forced to leave through a window, with the help of his servant, who happened to be nearby.

As editor, Street continued to arouse emotions. Eventually he was forced out of the newspaper business and moved to Illinois.[14] Soon he became active in local politics and joined the militia, where he rose to the rank of brigadier general. The militia was an integral part of society in the early days of the United States and was, from the very beginning, both a military and a political entity. In an era of penny-pinching politicians, the militia was a cheap substitute for a standing army. The militia operated on a democratic system of elections. Officers were elected by those in the ranks. Consequently, those who achieved high rank were usually prominent men, or men like Street, who were ambitious and looking for a way to enhance their stature in society.[15]

Though Street was successful in the local militia, he still needed a steady job. Street pressed his political friends, including Illinois governor Ninian Edwards, for a government appointment. When he heard about the vacancy at the Prairie du Chien agency, he lobbied for the job and was appointed there in 1827.[16]

Street argued with his superiors that both the Rock River and Fort Winnebago subagencies should be either eliminated or placed under his control. He likely resented that Kinzie was under Lewis Cass's jurisdiction and not William Clark's, as Street was. Street's animosity also may have stemmed from his longtime distrust of the American Fur Company. Street disapproved of the company's heavy-handed tactics and its unlimited use of whiskey to maintain its monopoly. Traders would often provide large quantities of alcohol during trade negotiations, resulting in deals that were very one-sided. The company's influence on Indian policy during treaty

negotiations alarmed Street, and he regularly
wrote to William Clark on the matter. Not
only did Kinzie have personal connections to the American Fur Company,
but he had also hired Pierre Paquette,
a company employee known for his
physical strength, humor, and hard
drinking, as his interpreter.

Kinzie's close association with
Cass also troubled Street. Cass
maintained close personal and
political relationships with the
American Fur Company and, un-
beknownst to many, was receiving large sums of cash from Astor.[17]
Cass's affiliation with the company is
best illustrated in the case of William

Joseph Street. WHI IMAGE ID 26632

Puthuff, the Indian agent at Mackinac Island who had the misfortune of
running afoul of the company in 1816. In the years immediately following
the War of 1812 it was illegal for British traders to engage in the fur trade
on American soil, regardless of what company they worked for. Astor had
many British nationals in his employ, some of whom had fought against
the United States during the war, and the law was proving a serious incon-
venience for him. Astor exerted his political muscle; through the secretary
of war, he had a letter sent to Puthoff and the local army commandant,
directing them to assist company officials at Mackinac in every way possible—meaning they should issue trade licenses to British nationals working
for Astor. Puthuff strongly opposed the directive and protested sharply to
Cass, who in turn ordered him to issue licenses to anyone Ramsey Crooks,
the chief of Astor's operations on the island, wanted. Unfortunately for
Puthoff, Cass's directives were known only by the territorial governor
and the agent. Puthoff was severely condemned by others in the Indian
department for his actions and in 1818 was removed from office.[18]

Street complained about the Fort Winnebago subagency for years. In
1833, he finally overreached when he sidestepped both Cass and Clark
and wrote directly to President Jackson recommending the removal of the

Fort Winnebago subagency. Cass, now secretary of war and Street's superior, tersely informed Street, "I do not coincide with the suggestion that a Sub-agent is not required at Fort Winnebago. I believe it is an important position, and that so long as the Indians remain in that region some officer must be there to have charge of their concerns."[19]

Street refrained from writing further letters. Kinzie, for his part, generally refrained from criticizing Street in his official correspondence—or at least if he did complain about Street, that correspondence hasn't survived. Perhaps it was enough that Kinzie had the unwavering support of Cass—support that continued after Cass was appointed secretary of war in 1831. But the tension between Street and Kinzie continued.

8

The Black Hawk War

When Kinzie wasn't making annuity payments or squabbling with his fellow agents, he was gathering information about the tribes in his region and reporting back to his superiors in Detroit and Washington. Kinzie's job as Indian agent was to be an observer, trying to determine the mood and possible actions of the Indians in his area. In 1832, the Black Hawk War would not only provide Kinzie with ample opportunity to report on his charges, it would also divide the Ho-Chunk, lead to the massive loss of Indian lands, and strain the relationship Kinzie had worked hard to create with the tribes at his agency.

Black Hawk was the leader of the defiant "British Band," an anti-American faction of Sauk and Meskwaki. In early April 1832, Black Hawk led his people across the Mississippi River to reclaim their village of Saukenuk, the longtime principal village of the tribe. The village, along with all of the tribe's remaining lands east of the Mississippi River, had been ceded to the United States in a treaty 1804. At the time, the US was not in a position to physically take control of its newly acquired territory, and though Congress ratified the treaty, the agreement was never fully accepted by the tribe.

In the subsequent twenty-eight years, the Sauk and Meskwaki remained on the land. Over time, some members of the tribe slowly emigrated west across the Mississippi River, leaving only the defiant British Band at Saukenuk. In June 1831 federal officials forced Black Hawk and his people to abandon the village. Ten months later, in April 1832, the British Band recrossed the Mississippi and occupied their old home.

Black Hawk's actions were more an act of defiance than an invasion, but federal officials and the white population of Illinois did not make that distinction. They remembered Black Hawk as a distinguished war leader who had fought alongside the British in the War of 1812. An army of militia and regular soldiers, led by Brigadier General Henry Atkinson, converged on the Sauk warrior and his band of people, compelling them to withdraw far up the Rock River and eventually deep into the Michigan Territory, in what is now Wisconsin.[1]

Atkinson notified Kinzie of Black Hawk's movements within weeks of the chief's crossing the Mississippi. On April 16, Atkinson wrote to Kinzie:

> You will inform the Winnebagoes of your agency of the movement of this Band of Sacs, and advise them to hold no intercourse with them. Any information you may acquire as to the location and conduct of the disaffected Sacs you will, communicate to me as early as possible, at Rock Island, also the temper and feelings of the Winnebagoes in relation to the subject.[2]

As the Black Hawk crisis escalated throughout that spring and summer, Kinzie held councils and informal talks with prominent leaders and warriors of both the Menominee and Ho-Chunk. He was in constant communication with numerous officials, passing on news that was coming into the fort.[3] Kinzie reported to Atkinson on June 7 that the Ho-Chunk "seem determined to prevent the hostile Indians from encroaching any further on their lands, and say they will kill everyone who shall cross the line of demarcation they intend to establish."[4]

It was tough talk, but not necessarily accurate. After fleeing Saukenuk, Black Hawk had tried to surrender, but to no avail. Instead his beleaguered band retreated farther to the north, hoping for support, or at the least protection, from the Ho-Chunk or Potawatomi.

Many Ho-Chunk tried to remain neutral in the Black Hawk War, while others provided outright assistance to the United States. The memory of the Winnebago War was still fresh, and many Ho-Chunk, most notably those living along the Mississippi River, were wary of supporting Black Hawk. On several occasions Black Hawk sent messengers to the Ho-Chunk along the Mississippi, inviting them to join him, and each time they refused.[5] For the Ho-Chunk living along the Wisconsin River, reaction to Black Hawk had as much to do with economics as with treaty obligations. Spoon Decorah, who lived near the portage, remembered years later, "Our sympathies were strongly with the whites. Our trading interests were with them, and we were bound to them by treaties."[6]

But the Rock River Band of Ho-Chunk aligned itself with Black Hawk. While the Ho-Chunk along the Mississippi had intermarried with the neighboring Dakota, who were longstanding Sauk enemies, the Rock River Ho-Chunk had intermarried with the Sauk. Of the sixteen Ho-Chunk leaders who had traveled to Washington with Kinzie in 1828, only one leader from the Rock River Band was among them and saw the cities, rode the canals, visited New York, and met with the president. In addition, the Rock River Ho-Chunk were the only ones to lose land in the Treaty of 1829. As a result they were the least impressed with the size and power of the Americans and had a natural sympathy for Black Hawk's cause.[7]

By early July 1832, after a series of isolated skirmishes, Black Hawk and his band took refuge around the vicinity of Lake Koshkonong, near present-day Fort Atkinson, Wisconsin. Supplies were running low, and starvation seemed imminent. When Black Hawk and his people left the area, General Atkinson briefly lost track of their whereabouts. The band's presence alarmed the inhabitants of Wisconsin, and the residents of Green Bay became especially apprehensive, as they feared the Sauk warrior might attempt an escape to Canada through their village.

—⊣⊢—

For Kinzie, the Black Hawk War created another problem: a growing refugee situation that was depleting the food supplies around the agency. After Black Hawk crossed the Mississippi River, fifty lodges of Ho-Chunk fled north and relocated to the area around the portage.[8] But these Ho-Chunk men were unfamiliar with the local terrain and were having little success with hunting. In mid-July 1832, Kinzie notified Governor George Porter that many Ho-Chunk were nearing starvation. Kinzie had been drawing upon stores from the fort, but those supplies were running short. Fort Winnebago was serving as a supply depot for operations against the Sauk, and Atkinson had just sent a large contingent of militia to the fort to retrieve provisions for his own army.[9]

The Black Hawk War never directly threatened the portage, yet Kinzie still took precautionary measures. In August 1832 he ordered his blacksmith shop at the Four Lakes (present-day Madison) dismantled and arranged for its equipment and supplies to be hidden, out of fear that the Rock River Ho-Chunk might destroy them.[10] The threat of war was serious enough for Kinzie to send his family north. On July 4, over Juliette's protests, he packed his family aboard a specially fitted boat and sent them to Green Bay. As it happened, Paquette was sending a boat of furs down the Fox River, which provided additional protection for Kinzie's family. Ironically, Kinzie sent his family to a community infused with panic. Rumors had swept Green Bay that Black Hawk was in the area. In addition, word had spread that cholera was following soldiers on their way to reinforce Fort Atkinson. Fortunately, though, neither Black Hawk nor the deadly disease would visit Green Bay that summer.

Juliette remained at Green Bay for two weeks, finding lodging at Fort Howard. Her traveling party included members of the extended Kinzie family and a young officer named David Hunter, who had married Kinzie's sister Maria in 1829. The group debated whether to catch the next schooner and continue on to Detroit or Chicago, but when a boat did come, with it came the news that cholera had broken out in both communities. With nowhere else to go, Juliette and her companions stayed at the fort, but they did not remain there for long. After about two weeks Juliette received a surprise visitor. Madame Four Legs, wife of the late chief and a friend of Juliette, arrived at Fort Howard with a letter from John. The militia companies under Colonel Dodge and Colonel James Henry, who had come to Fort Winnebago for supplies, had found Black Hawk's trail and had tracked him to the Wisconsin River. The militia attacked the British Band on July 21, but Black Hawk skillfully deflected their assaults long enough for his people to successful cross the river. Kinzie predicted the war would soon be over.[11]

Almost immediately, Juliette prepared to return to Fort Winnebago. Though the trip back started pleasantly enough, it turned out to be almost as perilous as the war they were meant to escape. At Grand Chute, near Appleton, Wisconsin, their boats pulled over to offload some cargo and passengers. Juliette and others in her boat thought it would be fun to run the rapids with the boatmen. The boat, however, ran against a tree jutting out from the riverbank and quickly sank. Juliette and her fellow passengers threw themselves against the nearest rocks and had to be pulled out of the river by David Hunter and several nearby Indians.[12] A few days later they arrived back at Fort Winnebago, a little worse for wear, but safe.

The war was rapidly approaching its inevitable and brutal end. Following the defensive action along the Wisconsin River, Black Hawk and his followers faced a grueling march over the rugged terrain of the southern Wisconsin uplands. Wracked with starvation and exhausted after months on the run, the British Band struggled through the valleys and bluffs to get to the Mississippi. Some of them broke away and fled down the Wisconsin River, while others collapsed and died along the march. Those who made it to the great river now had to figure out how to get across.

But their time had finally run out. Atkinson's army caught up with them on the banks of the Mississippi near the mouth of the Bad Axe River. On August 1 several members of the band built makeshift rafts and attempted to cross the river, but they were met by the steamboat *Warrior*, which was equipped with a small cannon. Black Hawk presented a white flag, but the captain of the boat believed it to be a ruse. The captain fired on the rafts, killing more than twenty of Black Hawk's people.

The next morning Atkinson's army launched its main attack. What started as an organized assault quickly spun out of control as Atkinson's soldiers swept the warriors and their families from the bluff tops and into the river. The few who managed to make it to the other side faced yet another deadly assault, this time from their old enemy the Dakota.

—ıı—

About eighty Ho-Chunk warriors from the Mississippi River area eventually served on the US side of the Black Hawk War under William S. Hamilton. Hamilton's company was a mixed command of Ho-Chunk, Dakota, and Menominee, charged with protecting the lead region and striking at isolated detachments of Black Hawk's band if the opportunity allowed. As Hamilton formed his company in Prairie du Chien, Street used the crisis to once again criticize Kinzie, writing to General Atkinson:

> Some efforts were made this morning by Winnebagoes runners from
> the Portage who have endeavoured to persuade the Inds. not to go, as
> Mr. Kinzie two day[s] past told the Winnebagoes not to hear what was

said by any white man, because he spoke to them the words of their
G.F. [Great Father]—and if any other man told them different it was
not right.[13]

But Street was taking Kinzie's comments completely out of context.
In reality, Kinzie was concerned that the Ho-Chunk of his area who were
decidedly neutral were being deliberately drawn into the conflict.[14] Kinzie
wrote to Governor Porter:

> I understand that some of the Winnebagoes of Genl. Street's Agency
> have consented to join Genl. Atkinson—I hope it may not be true; for
> the Winnebagoe nation is at peace with all the Ind. tribes, and I think
> it wrong that our people should excite them to war, when the greater
> part are anxious of remaining neutral, as they should do.[15]

Hamilton and his company never found an enemy to fight. Slowly
losing warriors who drifted away in frustration, Hamilton was eventually
left with twenty-five warriors to protect a small outpost near modern-day
Wiota, Wisconsin.[16]

Kinzie had his own problems with Atkinson that summer. The general's
shifting policy directives were aggravating. The subagent was doing all he
could to keep the Ho-Chunk neutral, only to be undermined by Atkinson,
who, during a council on June 11 with leaders from the Rock River Band,
implored the Ho-Chunk to "take up the Hatchet and join us . . . Keep the
Sacs deceived about everything til we are ready to strike them."[17] Kinzie
also believed Atkinson moved too slowly in chasing Black Hawk that summer and that the general's "tardy" movements led to many unnecessary
deaths in the mining district, including fellow Indian agent Felix St. Vrain,
who was reportedly killed by Sauk warriors earlier in May.[18] Had Kinzie
known the full story, he would have been even more concerned. Among
the war party that killed St. Vrain were a number of Ho-Chunk from the
Rock River Band.

9

THE AGENCY HOUSE

In June, as the Black Hawk War reached its fever pitch, Kinzie received official permission to build a new agency house. Kinzie had been requesting funds to build a more formal agency house for more than a year, but the news of the funding could not have come at a worse time. However, despite the war, Kinzie was determined to press ahead with the new home.

As a symbol of federal authority, an agency house could convey a message of power and importance to visiting chiefs, fur traders, and local citizens. The relative grandeur of an agency house also reflected the broader civil roles Indian agents often played in the community. For example, agents often served as justices of the peace or the local postmaster. Nicholas Boilvin, the agent at Prairie du Chien, was known to perform marriages. Other agencies, such as the one at Chicago, could serve as a voting hall during elections. Kinzie served as both a local magistrate and postmaster.[1] The house Kinzie built in the summer and fall of 1832 was substantial for the area but not unusual, given the homes of some of his contemporaries.

Agency houses were usually built near army posts, but some agents preferred to locate their facilities a prudent distance from the military. Some agents, most notably Lawrence Taliaferro and Henry Rowe Schoolcraft, avoided using quarters at their nearby forts, claiming that the Indians were more reluctant to visit them the closer they were to an army base.[2]

Agents and their families often had to use what was at hand. Some, like Henry Gratiot, simply used their own private residences as their agency houses. Charles Jouett, the Chicago agent who brought nine family members and servants with him when he received his appointment in 1817, noted bitterly to his superiors that the fourteen-foot-square agency house was little more than a hut with "but a single chair." Jouett complained to Lewis Cass that the officers at nearby Fort Dearborn were simply too busy to be concerned with his plight.[3]

When Alexander Wolcott replaced Jouett two years later, little had changed. A new agency house, which was started in Jouett's time, was in a rough state, a "mere shell," as Wolcott complained to his superiors.[4] Over the next few years Wolcott would change that, and his agency house evolved into a spacious and eccentric home called the "Cobweb Castle," probably named for the usual condition of the place as a result of Wolcott's solitary, bachelor lifestyle.

Similarly, Samuel C. Stambaugh found a dilapidated residence when he assumed control of the Green Bay agency in 1830:

> The house, when put in order, will be a very comfortable one, but it was in wretched plight as well as the lot upon which it stands.—I found it occupied by a family by the name of *Beale*, who were put in it this spring by the Agent. They left it a few days ago, as I wished to have some repairs made, which were *absolutely* necessary.[5]

In addition to the deplorable condition of Stambaugh's agency house, the location of the residences of the interpreter and the blacksmith made no sense. The agency was located on purchased land in an area still called the "private claims," while the interpreter lived two and a half miles up-river on government land. The blacksmith lived three miles below the river from the agency and in the opposite direction.[6]

Other agents succeeded in building substantial homes at the government's expense. Henry Row Schoolcraft, Indian agent at Sault Ste. Marie, boasted two magnificent homes during his career. At first Schoolcraft lived and presided out of his father-in-law's house, but after five years of lobbying, he received approval from the war department to build an agency house. "Elmwood," completed in 1827, was a stately home of no fewer than fifteen rooms. The elegant manor stood on a hill overlooking the St. Mary's River and its falls. Hardwoods and shade trees filled the spacious lawn. The entrance hall was a museum containing mineral specimens that harked back to the days when Schoolcraft was a mineralogist, various Indian artifacts, and taxidermy. The home was tastefully decorated with wallpaper, carpet, and furniture, leaving one visitor to remark that it was better than many similar dwellings in New England. Schoolcraft entertained equally lavishly, serving guests sumptuous banquets of more than eight meats, vegetables, desserts, breads, and a wide assortment of refreshments.[7]

Kinzie's nemesis, Joseph Street, first lived in the house of his predecessor, Nicholas Boilvin, next door to Fort Crawford. It was a crude house, about sixty by twenty-five feet in size and covered with bark. Reflecting the functional and self-sufficient nature of many agencies, Street's compound contained a detached kitchen, a milk house, a "spacious garden," and an additional thirty-by-twenty-five-foot structure that may have been used as a storehouse. Within a few years, Street moved inland to the mouth of Mill Coulee, near property owned by Joseph Rolette. By the time of the Black Hawk War, he had moved yet again, to a house he commissioned just north of the new Fort Crawford.[8]

The Indian agency at St. Peters, as Taliaferro would have one believe, was a squalid post wholly unsuited to the needs of the agent. It's true that his first building was a dismal affair, an old structure once used by a post sutler. After the house was washed away by floods in 1823, Taliaferro was able to erect a large, eighty-by-eighteen-foot, two-story stone and log house that included a hexagonal council chamber on the second floor with flags, pipes, and other gifts the various Native leaders had given him. The house was used as the private residence for Taliaferro and his staff, which by 1830 included a subagent and personal servants. The St. Peters agency would eventually include separate homes for the subagent, a blacksmith, and at least one interpreter.[9]

There is no record of where Kinzie lived when he first arrived at Fort Winnebago in 1829, although it is possible he lived on or near the subagency grounds. Unlike some of his fellow agents, Kinzie enjoyed good relations with the officers of Fort Winnebago and had no problem using the fort for his personal living space. He and Juliette eventually shared half of the commanding officer's quarters and had two rooms, sixteen by twenty feet each, with a fireplace. An eight-foot-wide hallway connected their quarters with the commanding officer's billet. As Juliette would remember years later:

Our quarters were spacious, but having been constructed of the green
trees of the forest, cut down and sawed into boards by the hands of
the soldiers, they were considerably given to shrinking and warping,
thus leaving many a yawning crevice. Stuffing the cracks with cotton
batting, and pasting strips of papers over them, formed the employment of many a leisure hour.[10]

In the spring of 1831, the army shifted its units along the northern
frontier, and four companies of the Fifth Infantry moved into Fort Winnebago. The new garrison brought with it a new cadre of officers, some
of whom were married. The Kinzies gave up their quarters inside the fort
and moved across the Fox River to a log cabin on the hill.[11] At this stage of
development the agency consisted of a modified log barracks, a dairy, sta-
bles, and a smokehouse. The largest house in the complex belonged not to
the subagent, but rather to the interpreter, Pierre Paquette. At the bottom
of the hill was the blacksmith shop, and nearby were other small cabins
for "our Frenchmen," which may refer to laborers used at the subagency.[12]

The old log barracks provided a rough abode, but they weren't without
character. Juliette compared their new home to an "old stable" and wrote:

> The main building consisted of a succession of four rooms, no two of
> which communicated with each other, but each opened by a door into
> the outward air. A small window cut through the logs in front and
> rear, gave light to the apartment. An immense clay chimney for every
> two rooms, occupied one side of each, and the ceiling overhead was
> composed of a few rough boards laid upon the transverse logs that
> supported the roof. It was surprising how soon a comfortable, home-
> like air was given to the old dilapidated rooms, by a few Indian mats
> spread upon the floor, the piano and other furniture ranged in their
> appropriate places, and even a few pictures hung against the logs.[13]

The crude log structure would not last long. In December 1830, Kinzie
requested four hundred dollars to build a home for the blacksmith and an
additional fifteen hundred for an agency house. The next spring funds
were approved for the blacksmith residence. As luck would have it, the
smithy, a bachelor, was then boarding with a friend and was willing to let

Kinzie stay in the new house. Juliette and John took the opportunity to design the home to suit their tastes. It was a simple structure with a kitchen, two bedrooms, and a parlor on the first floor and two "low chambers" on the second. It was not a fancy establishment, but it would do until Congress appropriated funds for a more formal home.[14]

When Kinzie finally received permission to build a new agency house, he chose a location that was at once under the watchful eye of the garrison while at the same time some distance away. The grounds, however, held significance for the local tribe. Archaeological evidence suggests that both sides of the Fox River had been the site of villages going back centuries.[15] The choice for the location of the building site was an interesting one. As Juliette noted, the new agency house was built on a site that had "some very unsightly pickets surrounding two or three Indian graves, on the esplanade in front of the house."[16] Both husband and wife were aware of the sensitivity of doing anything with the graves.

> Accordingly a little structure about a foot in height, properly finished with a moulding around the edge, was substituted for the worn and blackened pickets, and it was touching to witness the mournful satisfaction with which two or three old crones would come regularly every evening at sunset, to sit and gossip over the ashes of their departed relatives. On the fine, moonlight nights too, there might often be seen a group sitting there, and enjoying what is to them a solemn hour, for they entertain the poetic belief that "the moon was made to give light to the dead."[17]

Romantic as the scene may have been, the Kinzies were building their new agency house on a known burial ground. The site was significant enough to be the final resting place of Four Legs, who died near Fort Winnebago in the fall of 1830 and was buried on the hill behind the agency house.[18]

Building the new house was not an easy undertaking. Alexander McComb, the commanding general of the army, had informed Cass that Kinzie could use soldiers from the fort to build the new house as long as they were not needed by the fort commandant. Unfortunately for Kinzie, Captain Plympton could not spare any of his men. "Mechanicks" had to be brought in from as far away as St. Louis, prompting Kinzie to later complain, "It was with great difficulty that I succeeded in getting them, as the Indian war, which had just commenced, operated greatly against me."

The project also included the construction of a new outhouse easily accessible from the back door by the kitchen. Built on a stone foundation, the structure was a timber frame lined with bricks made locally at a brickyard along the Wisconsin River. Lumber was shipped from Green Bay or cut along the Wisconsin River more than seventy miles above the portage. Despite the difficulties, Kinzie could report that the building was constructed as cheaply as possible, and even the lumber contractor provided the necessary timber at a loss.[19]

When it was completed, the agency house was an imposing structure for central Wisconsin. It was not as extravagant as Schoolcraft's Elmwood, nor as imposing as Taliaferro's council house, but it was still an elegant home. Visitors entered through a narrow vestibule. A set of stairs immediately to the left led to the private family chambers on the second floor. The downstairs contained four rooms. A main room, or parlor, to the right of the main entrance was most likely Kinzie's office. A doorway on the west wall led to a dining room. A small room, perhaps a storeroom, led off to one side of the dining room. At the back of the house was a comfortably sized kitchen. The second level boasted four bedrooms and an additional storeroom or servant's chamber at the back of the house.

The construction of the new home came just in time, as the Kinzie household was becoming a crowded affair. The previous year, Kinzie's mother, sister Maria and her son, brother Robert, and the family's servants moved from Chicago to the portage. Kinzie's father had died several years before. In April 1832 Juliette became pregnant with their first child. The agency was a lively place, and in January 1833 things only became livelier with the arrival of a son, Alexander Wolcott Kinzie. The Kinzies continued to enjoy good relations with the officers of the fort, and it was not uncommon for officers' wives to gather at the agency house. Juliette often entertained guests by playing her piano, which she had transported with great care from Detroit. John added to the festivities by pulling out his violin.

Charlotte Ouisconsin Van Cleve, the wife of an officer of the fort, remembered years later, "The memory of the weekly musicals at John Kinzie's pleasant agency, and the delightful rides on horseback over the portage to the point where Portage City nowstands, quickens my heart even now."[20]

For Van Cleve it was a bucolic scene, but it would not last. Within months of the new agency house's completion, the Kinzie family would leave the portage forever.

10

LEAVING THE PORTAGE

Kinzie had his hands full in the spring and summer of 1832. A growing family, building the new agency house, and struggling with the crisis of the Black Hawk War would be enough for any Indian agent. In May, Congress added to his burdens when it passed an act providing for the vaccinations of various Indian tribes against smallpox. Kinzie now had to figure his way through the grisly process of inoculating hundreds of Ho-Chunk. And the end of the summer would see yet another treaty council and even more hardships for the Ho-Chunk living around Fort Winnebago.

The Vaccination Act of May 5, 1832, marked the first time Congress passed a law governing health care for Native Americans. The act provided "the means of extending the benefits of vaccination, as a preventative of smallpox, to the Indian tribes, and therefore as far as possible, to save them from the destructive ravages of that disease."[1] Congress was responding to the alarming epidemic sweeping through the tribes on the western frontier. Officials in Washington had received reports of the epidemic for some time. Agents and missionaries were pleading for assistance, and prior to 1832 an unofficial vaccination program had actually been implemented.[2]

The act was a controversial measure. Its primary opposition came from southern members of the Senate, who argued that the project was too expensive, or that it was helping a people considered enemies of the United States.[3]

There is also some suggestion that the act was motivated by the newly formalized policy of Indian removal. The Indian Removal Act of May 28, 1830, was a centerpiece of Andrew Jackson's legislative agenda. It authorized the president to engage in a spree of treaty negotiations aimed at eliminating all Native American presence east of the Mississippi. Jackson personally believed the best way to preserve the tribes as they existed and to ensure the security of the nation was to remove them, peaceably, to lands west of the great river.[4] The reality of Jackson's policies was quite different. Regardless of his motivations, Jackson was also excessively frugal. He is the only president to have paid off the national debt; but to do so, many of his programs were underfunded. Jackson also had a volatile personality that others were hesitant to cross. Consequently, his removal policy was a humanitarian disaster, as evidenced by the Cherokee Trail of Tears and the near-decade-long Second Seminole War.

Like the Vaccination Act, the Removal Act was passed only after considerable debate and was as much the product of Jackson's will as anything else. Jackson had spent much of his young adult life fighting Indians in the south, on the Tennessee frontier and during the War of 1812. He had dealt with a federal government that exercised an Indian policy that was vague, indecisive, and often dangerous to the safety of the nation as he saw it. When he became president in 1829, Jackson was determined to redefine federal Indian policy; to him, removal was an important step in that direction. The spreading of smallpox, however, threatened to delay the removal process. It was more difficult to remove the eastern tribes to the west if that region was experiencing an epidemic.[5]

Jackson's vaccination policy had economic ramifications as well, in that the smallpox epidemic threatened white settlers' ability to trade with the Indians. The experience of Jacques Vieau reflected that of many along the frontier. Vieau, a fur trader in the Milwaukee area, was nearly ruined as a result of smallpox in the winter of 1832–33. Vieau's son Andrew recollected:

> Father and his crew were busy throughout the winter in burying the Natives, who died like sheep with the foot-rot. With a crooked stick inserted under the dead Indian's chin they would haul the infected corpse into a shallow pit dug for its reception and give it a hasty burial. In this work, and in assisting the poor wretches who survived, my father lost much time and money; while of course none of the Indians who lived over, were capable of paying their debts to the traders.[6]

The vaccination act required each Indian agent to oversee the vaccination of Indians in his care. This meant the acquisition of vaccine matter and the hiring of a doctor, often from a nearby army post, to administer it. The situation was more complicated for John Kinzie. Congress allocated only twelve thousand dollars to cover the program nationwide. Consequently, many army surgeons, including the one at Fort Winnebago, refused to assist because the cost to administer the vaccines exceeded the amount they would be reimbursed. This was not the first time Kinzie had had problems with the post surgeon. Kinzie had complained to Cass, "Many Indians come to me for medical aid, and the Physician at the post will not, except in extreme cases, prescribe for them."[7] Kinzie himself was hesitant to take his own family to the post surgeon. In the fall of 1831, when his mother was ill, Kinzie felt it was better to make a journey to Fort Crawford at Prairie du Chien to see his old friend Dr. Beaumont.[8]

The situation convinced Kinzie of the need for a physician at the agency under his own direction, independent of the army surgeon at the fort. During treaty negotiations later that August at Rock Island, Kinzie successfully secured an annual appropriation of two hundred dollars for a physician at both Fort Winnebago and Prairie du Chien. This would be the first known instance of a tribe in the US receiving a federally funded physician as dictated by a treaty.[9]

But it would be more than a year before a doctor would be appointed, so that summer Kinzie was compelled to administer the vaccinations himself. The vaccination process wasn't pleasant. First, the administrator had to collect "matter" from the swelling pustules of patients already infected. Then, to vaccinate healthy patients, he had to insert the infected matter under the patients' skin. Inevitably infections would follow, from either the vaccination process or a mild outbreak of the disease itself. If the patient survived the vaccination process, he or she had a better chance of surviving the next epidemic.[10]

Kinzie was fortunate to receive precollected matter from St. Louis; however, he still had to perform the vaccinations. The agent sought out Paquette, whom the tribe trusted, to help administer the matter.[11] The procedure must have been ghastly to watch and the subsequent infections difficult to deal with. Together, Kinzie and Paquette treated at least six hundred Ho-Chunk at the agency.[12]

In late August, as soon as they had completed administering the vaccinations, Kinzie received a letter from General Winfield Scott demanding that Kinzie send all the leaders of the nearby Ho-Chunk to Rock Island, Illinois. The war against the Sauk was over, and Scott and Illinois governor John Reynolds were convening a council with the Sauk and Meskwaki, Dakota, Menominee, and Ho-Chunk. Their initial intent was to conclude a formal peace ending the summer's conflict. But in the weeks following the cataclysmic battle at Bad Axe, information streamed in to Scott from several sources suggesting that the Ho-Chunk were more involved with Black Hawk than had been generally known. Scott was calling in every available tribal leader and intended to conduct an investigation.[13]

In a lengthy letter to Cass, Winfield Scott laid out the case against the Ho-Chunk. "The evidence of many prisoners, examined apart from each other, may be considered as conclusive as to certain acts of hostility committed by the Winnebagoes," he wrote. Scott went on to detail correspondence from Samuel Stambaugh, who had led two companies of Menominee warriors that summer and who claimed, "These people [the Ho-Chunk] attempted at every point we met them, on our route from Green Bay to the Prairie, to prevent the Menominies from going to war against the Sacs; said the Americans were enemies of all red men, & that the Sacs would yet be victorious."[14]

Stambaugh's correspondence and his subsequent activities rounding up any remaining Sauk fugitives, including those suspected to be hiding among the Ho-Chunk near Fort Winnebago, led Scott to believe the Ho-Chunk were more in collusion with Black Hawk than the tribe was claiming. Scott had apparently originally intended to require that only the Rock River Ho-Chunk attend the council, but now he summoned all of the tribe, including those living at the portage.

Kinzie had not planned to attend the council. He had been preparing to travel to Green Bay to pick up that year's annuity payments, but after the chiefs asked that he accompany them, he changed his mind.[15] Once again, the divided nature of the Ho-Chunk affected matters. Certainly the tribe was split during the war, but this division was exacerbated by Joseph Street, who was, perhaps, trying to save his own reputation. Recent criticism aimed at Street insinuated that Indians of his agency aided Black Hawk. Street, however, asserted that those who helped Black Hawk were not of his agency but from the bands south of the Wisconsin, namely the Rock River Ho-Chunk.[16]

The Rock River Band was represented at the council by White Crow, the same leader who had effectively manipulated negotiations at the 1828 council at Green Bay, successfully delaying land cessions for a year. The chief admitted the complicity of his tribe but also pointed to numerous instances where Ho-Chunk had assisted the United States, including the protection of Henry Gratiot and the rescue of hostages. General Scott, though impressed by White Crow's oratory, still forced the tribe to cede 2.5 million acres of land to the United States as punishment for their involvement in the Black Hawk War. Effectively all remaining tribal lands south and east of the Wisconsin River would be given up. In exchange, the tribe would receive an annual annuity of ten thousand dollars for twenty-seven years and a school built near Prairie du Chien.[17]

The treaty provided the Ho-Chunk with new lands in Iowa dubbed the "neutral territory," a sliver of land wedged between the Dakota and their Sauk and Meskwaki enemies. The Ho-Chunk were presented with two options: move west to the neutral territory, or move north of the Wisconsin River. Elbert Herring, commissioner of Indian affairs, knew the choice to move west would be a difficult one for the Ho-Chunk to make. Still, Herring believed no alternative was possible, and he considered future moves west to be inevitable.[18] He wrote: "The well-known hostility of the Sioux [Dakota] and Sacs to the Winnebagoes may perhaps indicate the expediency of keeping them wide apart, but even with that discouraging circumstance, the resulting benefit from their removal west would in my opinion, far outweigh all possible injury."[19]

While attending the treaty council, Kinzie was exposed to cholera. An epidemic of the disease had been sweeping eastward across the country and had prevented General Scott from taking command of the war effort because of a quarantine at Chicago. When Kinzie arrived at the council, Scott directed him to land his delegation on the north end of the island to avoid the cholera-stricken encampment. Yet Kinzie fell ill on the trip home. Paquette, who had been traveling with Kinzie, took him to a nearby cabin and spent the next few weeks nursing Kinzie back to health.

The Treaty of 1832 and its aftermath would come to dominate Kinzie's final months as agent. Kinzie, Gratiot, and Street were all directed to encourage the tribe to move west and to provide any assistance and provisions necessary. The Ho-Chunk had little time to consider their options. They were to remove from the ceded territory by June 1, 1833.

As the Ho-Chunk struggled to come to grips with the harsh realities of removal, Kinzie reported another problem facing tribal leaders: food. For the second time in less than a year the Ho-Chunk Nation was facing a critical food shortage. Fort Winnebago had been a supply depot during the Black Hawk War, but the increased presence of regular soldiers and militia as well as the subsequent refugee crisis depleted existing supplies. The war had also disrupted the summer growing season, and the Ho-Chunk were not able to harvest much of their own crops. The winter of 1832–33 brought additional problems. In March 1833, Kinzie reported to Governor Porter that the lack of snow that winter and spring had made it difficult to track game, and the Ho-Chunk had not been able to kill enough deer or bear to supplement their diet. The tribe members were reduced to living on whatever they could find, in at least one instance making stew out of bark and acorns. Kinzie issued food whenever he could, but as the winter months depleted the commissary stores of Fort Winnebago, the post commandant cut off even that source.[20]

In the fall of 1832 Kinzie anticipated the looming food shortage. He requisitioned corn from Fort Howard, only to be told there was no available corn in Green Bay or eastern Michigan. The nearest stockpile was in Ohio. By the time the corn was purchased, it was winter and the Fox River had frozen over.[21] Only when the river opened again the next spring did the supply boats arrive. As ever, Juliette was there to record the scene of the boat's arrival:

> The announcement, at length, that "the boats were in sight," was a
> thrilling and most joyful sound. Hundreds of poor creatures were
> at once assembled on the bank, watching their arrival. Oh! how tor-
> turing was their slow approach, by the winding course of the river,
> through the extended prairie! As the first boat touched the bank,
> we, who were gazing on the scene with anxiety and impatience
> only equalled by that of the sufferers, could scarcely refrain from
> laughing.[22]

The severity of the winter weighed heavily on the leaders of the tribe. The arrival of the supply boats had ended the hunger, but there was still the impending removal. Resigned to the reality that they would have to vacate their lands east of the Wisconsin, the Ho-Chunk implored Kinzie in March to delay the move for another year. One more growing season would provide them with enough corn to make it through the following winter, in the event the hunting season was again bad. Kinzie supported the idea and passed on the request to Governor Porter, pointing out that the request came from Ho-Chunks living in the Lake Winnebago and Green Lake region, a section of the tribe that "are peaceable Indians, and have not to my knowledge committed any depredations, upon any White Person since I have been among them."[23] But Herring was adamant, writing to Porter in late March, "The Winnebagoes shall leave the ceded country on or before the first day of June."[24]

The War Department, anticipating difficulty, called in Colonel Henry Dodge of the US Dragoons to convince the tribe to move across the Mississippi River. The Ho-Chunk resistance to removal was incomprehensible to Dodge. After holding a talk with the tribe in May 1833 at which both Kinzie and Gratiot were present, Dodge reported that there was a "great unwillingness on the part of the Winnebagoes to leave the country they have ceded to the United States." Dodge complained, "The Winnebagoes are the most difficult Indians to understand I have ever been acquainted with; there is a stubborn sulkiness of disposition about them that I don't entirely know what it originates from."[25] In truth, Herring had written that it was up to the Ho-Chunk to determine where they would emigrate. To the dismay of federal officials, the bulk of the tribe elected to move north and by the end of June had settled along the Baraboo River and Portage in areas around Kinzie's agency. Yet, considering their options, the choice is not a surprise: move to a war zone between two enemy tribes, or relocate to the last parcel of tribal territory within the vicinity of a sympathetic Indian agent.

The Treaty of 1832 and the subsequent removal efforts should have suggested to Kinzie that the days of the Fort Winnebago subagency were numbered. And yet, writing to Territorial Governor Porter in October 1832, Kinzie was optimistic: "There is every reason to believe a full agency will be established here soon, and that it will be permanent. There are now more

Indians who visit this place, than any other within your Superintendency except Chicago."[26]

Lewis Cass and others felt the subagency was important, especially because of the removal process and the uncertainty of how the Ho-Chunk might respond to future removal efforts. It was equally clear, given Herring's assertions, that the Ho-Chunk would be asked to make further land cessions and eventually leave Wisconsin completely.[27]

Kinzie's optimism was misplaced. Budgetary constraints of a frugal Congress and president meant any upgrades to the agency were not going to be forthcoming. Commissioner

An illustration of Henry Dodge in 1834 as he would have appeared during the Black Hawk War. WHI IMAGE ID 27177

Herring noted to Porter in March that he would prefer to promote Kinzie's post to a full agency but only after "the discontinuance of any existing agency will furnish the opportunity."[28] Pay was also a factor, but as Herring noted, his compensation was set by statute. It was important to have someone to oversee Indian–white relations at the portage, but it was not important enough to Congress to justify the expenditure of paying for a full Indian agent.

In February 1833, Kinzie traveled to Chicago with his friend and brother-in-law Lieutenant David Hunter, and probably his brother Robert Kinzie, to lay out lots and streets for the city's "Kinzie Addition." Chicago was a growing distraction for the subagent. The lakeshore village had always been his home, but now it was also on the verge of a development explosion, and the Kinzie family held a large parcel of valuable land near the mouth of the Chicago River.[29]

Perhaps the allure of a potentially lucrative real estate business may have led Kinzie to rethink his future. Five months later, on July 1, 1833, he submitted his resignation to Governor Porter. The move took some by surprise. Kinzie's rationale for leaving isn't clear. Kinzie's correspondence that spring doesn't suggest he was planning to leave. Governor Porter characterized Kinzie's departure as abrupt. Even Juliette does not make any mention of her husband's reasons in *Wau-Bun*.

Kinzie's own resignation letter is brief and does not offer any clues. Louise Phelps Kellogg, the eminent Wisconsin historian, has suggested that Kinzie was frustrated that his subagency and consequently his own rank would not be advanced.[30] Perhaps it was a growing sense of frustration with the job. He was constantly fighting fellow agents and businessmen while witnessing a steadily worsening situation for the Indians in his care. It is undeniable that matters were getting worse for the Ho-Chunk, and there was little he could do to help.

There were other distractions as well. Kinzie was also facing possible disciplinary action. In August 1832, as the Black Hawk War was coming to a close, Samuel Stambaugh leveled charges against Kinzie. Stambaugh, who was at the time in command of two companies of Menominee warriors, believed that Kinzie, in his capacity as postmaster at Fort Winnebago, had purposely held up important dispatches Stambaugh had sent to General Atkinson the previous spring.[31] Kinzie was aware of the charges, but he didn't know at the time whether they had come from Stambaugh or Street. Writing to Governor Porter in March 1833, Kinzie speculated, "Some kind friend of mine has addressed a letter to Mr. Herring, making sundry charges against me for want of seal etc. in relation to the late Indian disturbances. I know of none who could have been so kind, except my friend the *Menominee Warrior* [Kinzie's emphasis] who is now Secty: to some Commissioners, or my *brother chiefs* at the Prairie du Chien."[32]

Stambaugh had made waves before. Shortly after his arrival at Green Bay two years earlier, Stambaugh had investigated Judge Doty's land speculation deals and possible conflicts of interest. Stambaugh's investigation helped remove Doty from the bench as the additional judge of Michigan Territory. But in Kinzie's case, Stambaugh's charges were likely unfair. Mail was notoriously slow and inefficient in the territory, and even Kinzie noted the slow delivery that spring before the outbreak of war.

Whether it was a lack of advancement, a desire to avoid an investigation, or simply frustration with a darkening situation for the Ho-Chunk,

Kinzie left the portage that July. The Ho-Chunk were dismayed when they heard the news, as Juliette later remembered:

The intelligence, when communicated to our Winnebago children, brought forth great lamentations and demonstrations of regret. From the surrounding country they came flocking in, to inquire into the truth of the tidings they had heard, and to petition earnestly that we would continue to live and die among them.[33]

But the pleas of the Ho-Chunk were to no avail. The Kinzie family boarded mackinaw boats and traveled down the Fox River, where they caught a steamer for Chicago. Juliette recorded how they felt in the moment of their departure:

It was with sad hearts that on the morning of the 1st of July, 1833, we bade adieu to the long cortege which followed us to the boat, now waiting to convey us to Green Bay, where we were to meet Governor Porter and Mr. Brush, and proceed, under their escort, to Detroit. When they had completed their tender farewells, they turned to accompany their father across the Portage, on his route to Chicago, and long after, we could see them winding along the road, and hear their loud lamentations at a parting which they foresaw would be forever.[34]

The Fort Winnebago subagency would continue for a number of years, but it would never be quite the same, nor would it have an agent as experienced or motivated as John Kinzie. In September Robert McCabe, a major in the US Army, was appointed subagent at the portage and took up residency at the agency house. Like many other new agents, McCabe was unprepared for the job, but he was also unnecessarily handicapped from the start. When Kinzie left the portage, he turned over all the official papers, including treaty books, regulations, forms, and vouchers, to Robert Irwin, a former Indian factor at Green Bay, who assumed duties of acting agent. However, Irwin unexpectedly died several days after taking over the agency. Governor Porter presumed the agency documents were passed on to the commandant of Fort Winnebago, Lieutenant Colonel Enos Cutler.

Though McCabe eventually found the papers, he wrote to the territorial governor in exasperation at not having any instructions about his job.[35]

McCabe's tenure was even briefer than Kinzie's. Within a year he resigned, after a severe bout of palsy. A reorganization of the Indian Department in 1834 required that in the absence of an Indian agent, the job could be delegated to an army officer. In the summer of 1834, Lieutenant Colonel Cutler was informed that he was now assuming the duties of the local agent. Annuity payments would be handled by his quartermaster, but all responsibility for the payments rested with him. Cutler complained about the additional workload in a letter to the governor, but to no avail.[36]

For the next eleven years Fort Winnebago would see no fewer than eight commanding officers rotate through the post. The continuity and quality of the agency suffered. Within ten years, the importance of the agency and the fort declined. By 1840, the primary function of the garrison and the subagency was to remove the Ho-Chunk from Wisconsin. In 1845, the buildup for the Mexican War siphoned off the remaining solders from the post; and twelve years after Kinzie left the portage, Fort Winnebago and its Indian agency closed their doors.

11

CHICAGO

When Kinzie and his family landed at Chicago, they discovered the tiny frontier community swelling with thousands of Indians, traders, and government officials. And once again, Kinzie found himself involved in yet another treaty council. But this time, it was not as an agent of the federal government, but rather as a private entrepreneur.

That summer Governor Porter was convening a council at Chicago with the Ojibwe, Ottawa, and Potawatomi. Porter's principal goal was to purchase title to all remaining Indian lands in Illinois. Pressure for additional land cessions in the state had been constant since the summer of 1827. The Winnebago War had created a poisonous anti-Indian atmosphere that affected many of the tribes of the upper Midwest. Despite the Potawatomi's neutrality that summer, Illinois governor Ninian Edwards and other federal and state officials used the uprising of 1827 as a pretext to call for the tribe's removal. During the Black Hawk War, Illinois officials maintained strong suspicions that the Potawatomi were involved, even though their own agent, Thomas Owen, insisted that the tribe had not participated.[1]

The Chicago treaty, signed on September 26, 1833, had far-reaching consequences for everyone in the Chicago area. It permanently eliminated the Native presence from the region and prompted the development that would turn the small fur-trading community of Chicago into the largest metropolis in the Midwest.

The treaty would have no less an impact on the Kinzie family, who were among the many individuals and companies who submitted more than 350 claims against the tribes. Traders, local businessmen, and families came forward, demanding payment for a wide variety of grievances, some going as far back as the War of 1812. One notable claimant was Robert Stuart, Kinzie's old boss from his days on Mackinac Island. Stuart was there to ensure that the American Fur Company received $17,000 for old trade debts and various damages the Potawatomi had inflicted on company property over the years. Stuart succeeded, in both his claim and his attempt to secure money from the Kinzie family for debts John Sr. owed the company from his days as a fur trader, when he bought supplies on credit. Part of Stuart's debt was paid out of the $26,500 the Kinzie family received for damages suffered as a result of the Battle of Fort Dearborn.[2]

In addition, Governor Porter awarded substantial contracts to local businessmen to provide various goods and supplies to be delivered during the treaty council. These were most likely provisions, various trade goods, and horses. Kinzie received one of these contracts, as did Gholson Kercheval, who briefly served as Indian agent at Chicago after the death of Alexander Wolcott in 1831. Together, Kinzie and Kercheval provided one hundred thousand dollars' worth of goods at a 50 percent markup, resulting in a combined profit of fifty thousand dollars. In awarding these contracts, Porter sidestepped normal procedure, as the distribution of supplies during treaty councils was normally handled by the local Indian agent. Porter's apparent favoritism of Kinzie, Kercheval, and others did not go unnoticed. A few months later, in December 1833, the Senate Committee on Indian Affairs launched an investigation. This could have posed a problem for Kinzie, but Porter's death from cholera in 1834 put an end to the matter.[3]

The Chicago treaty provided Kinzie with financial reserves, and his longtime family association with the city had resulted in substantial land holdings. The lands surrounding the Kinzie family home included approximately 102 acres of prime real estate in the heart of what would later become downtown Chicago. The "Kinzie Addition," as the section would be called, stretched from the north bank of the Chicago River to West Chicago Avenue, and from Lake Michigan to North State Street. With the Erie Canal completed and shipping on the Great Lakes on the rise, Chicago was rapidly developing. By 1837, four years after the Kinzies returned and the treaty was signed, Chicago was incorporated as a city with more than four thousand inhabitants. Kinzie was in the right place at the right time.

—||—

Chicago in 1833 as the Kinzie family would have known it. CHICAGO HISTORY MUSEUM, ICHI
05946; HERRIOT, JUSTIN B., CREATOR

For Kinzie's former charges, the years following his departure from the
portage were increasingly grim. The treaty at Rock Island would not be the
federal government's final attempt to acquire tribal lands. When Kinzie
left Fort Winnebago, the Ho-Chunk still retained territory north and west
of the Wisconsin River, and the vast majority of the tribe remained in
their native region, establishing villages along the Wisconsin and Baraboo
Rivers. Yet between 1832 and 1836, the United States continued its efforts
to eliminate all Ho-Chunk title to lands in Wisconsin. Each year, as the
leaders of the tribe arrived at Fort Crawford or Fort Winnebago to receive
their annuity payments, they were pressed to sell more land by the Indian
agents and commissioners, including Henry Dodge, who would be named
governor of the newly created Wisconsin Territory in 1836.

For a time, the tribe held out and refused all offers for their lands.[4]
Then, in the fall of 1837, Dodge invited the Ho-Chunk to send a delegation
to Washington, DC, to meet with President Martin Van Buren. Tribal leaders asked why the trip was necessary, but Dodge was evasive, saying only

that it was an opportunity to become acquainted with the newly elected president and to receive gifts.[5]

The Ho-Chunk suspected they would be asked to cede more land, so they assembled a delegation of twenty chiefs who had no authority to sell. The tribe's fears were well-founded. Once the Ho-Chunk delegation reached the capital, US commissioners informed the chiefs that they wanted to purchase all the remaining tribal territory in Wisconsin. When the chiefs flatly refused, the commissioners threatened to keep them from their homes until they relented. Scared of never seeing their families again and hoping to secure time to renegotiate a better deal, the chiefs finally agreed to sign the treaty, with the stipulation that the tribe could remain in Wisconsin for eight years before being forced to move to the neutral grounds.[6]

Documents are sketchy about what happened next. Apparently the interpreters at the negotiations told the chiefs they would have eight years, but when the commissioners drafted the agreement, the time allotted was reduced to eight months.[7] Once the group returned to Wisconsin, it would in fact take three years to orchestrate the first removal effort, as soldiers from Fort Winnebago traveled across the surrounding countryside, gathering the scattered bands and sending them to Iowa.

One year after the Ho-Chunk chiefs were forced to sign the Washington treaty, Kinzie returned to the portage to help distribute the treaty's annuity payments, possibly at the request of Henry Dodge, who was not only governor, but also superintendent of Indian affairs for the Wisconsin Territory. While back in Wisconsin, Kinzie had a private conversation with Dandy, a Ho-Chunk chief from the Lake Winnebago area. Dandy was an outspoken critic of the latest treaty; he spoke freely about his dissatisfaction and his strong disapproval of members of the tribe who were complying with their forced removal. Dandy was intent on remaining in Wisconsin and suggested to Kinzie that others of the tribe felt the same way. Kinzie reported the conversation in detail to Dodge.[8] It's difficult to reconcile Kinzie's decision to betray Dandy's confidence, given his reputation for sympathy for the tribe. But Kinzie knew Dodge well, and perhaps he was acting out of a sense of loyalty to an old friend.

The years from 1837 to 1874 were a perilous period for the Ho-Chunk. The Washington treaty of 1837 ended any legal title the tribe had in Wisconsin, and despite Dandy's assertions that many were determined to stay, the tribe had little choice but to move to the "neutral ground" set aside for them in Iowa. The first wave of Ho-Chunk were forced from Wisconsin and moved to the new territory in 1840. But life in between the warring Dakota and their Sauk and Meskwaki enemies was unbearable. In 1846 the tribe again sold their lands in the neutral ground and moved first to western Minnesota and later to Nebraska.

In 1850 the federal government attempted to gather up the few disparate groups of Ho-Chunk who remained in Wisconsin. But here, Dandy was correct—there were a few among the tribe who were determined to stay. In what later became Sauk County, two Ho-Chunk leaders, Wakabjaziga, or Yellow Thunder, and Blue Wing, whose Ho-Chunk name is unknown, each took the unusual step of purchasing forty acres of land as US citizens.[9] Their parcels attracted others, and for several years this land became a gathering place for Ho-Chunk determined to remain in their homeland.

With each passing year, small groups of Ho-Chunk migrated back to Wisconsin. Often they could be found living in backwood ravines and remote swampy areas. The local white population either aided the impoverished people or demanded their removal.[10] For forty years the army rounded up the scattered bands and shipped them out west, only to have to do it again a few years later. In 1875 an amendment of the Homestead Act included a provision allowing the Ho-Chunk to remain in Wisconsin. But those who stayed had no territory they could call their own. Even today the Ho-Chunk Nation does not have a formal reservation in Wisconsin.

—⊩—

Helping with the annuity payments in 1838 was the last interaction Kinzie had with the Office of Indian Affairs. He had more pressing business to deal with in Chicago. In addition to revenue from land sales in the Kinzie Addition, the financial income from Governor Porter's Chicago treaty of 1833 enabled Kinzie to set up business as a forwarding and commissioning agent, a form of broker or purchasing agent. He also maintained a warehouse of hardware supplies, including window sashes, nails, glass, and salt, that he sold to builders, and he also dabbled in lumber.[11] Later he formed a partnership with his brother in-law, David Hunter, and his old friend Gurdon Hubbard, and founded the Illinois Transportation Line, a wagon business that hauled freight between Chicago, Peru, and Utica.[12] And in 1835 Kinzie established himself in the banking industry as president of Chicago's first bank, a branch of the State Bank of Illinois.[13]

As his businesses thrived, Kinzie developed a taste for politics. In 1834 he was elected second president of the village of Chicago. In 1837 Kinzie ran for mayor in the first election held by the newly incorporated city, but he lost to William B. Ogden. Though he was unlucky at the polls, Kinzie still found a way to serve in a number of public roles. In 1839 he was serving as an election judge for the Sixth Ward, and by 1843 he was appointed register of the land office, a federal position that he held for many years.[14]

The Kinzies would also take a leading role in Chicago's religious community. Religion always played an important role in their family life, especially for Juliette, who was a devout Episcopalian. Traveling bishops were always welcome at the family home, and Juliette's activities earned her the unofficial title of "Female Bishop of Illinois."[15] Shortly after relocating to Chicago, Kinzie and his old friend Gurdon Hubbard were among those who formed St. James Church, the first Episcopalian congregation in the village. Kinzie later donated two lots for a church building that was completed by 1837.

Though now Kinzie was an urban businessman, his days in the wilderness continued to follow him, although often his experience served to entertain those around him. Once on a boat trip to Mackinaw Island, he was pressed by his fellow travelers to perform an "Indian dance and song."[16] Perhaps it was similar to a performance observed by the eminent English writer Harriet Martineau, then traveling through the United States. Martineau was invited to dinner at the Kinzies' home while on her way through Chicago. She was impressed by the family's respect for Native Americans, noting that "they were the only persons I met who, really knowing the Indians, had any regard for them. The testimony was universal to the good faith, and other virtues of savage life of the unsophisticated Indians; but they were spoken of in tone of dislike, as well as pity, by all but this family, and they certainly had studied their Indian neighbors very thoroughly."[17]

Later in the evening Kinzie and his brother Robert performed for their guests, as Martineau described:

> We had the fearful pleasure of seeing various savage dances performed by the Indian agent and his brother with the accompaniments

of complete costume, barbaric music, and whooping. The most intelligible to us was the Discovery Dance, a highly descriptive pantomime. We saw the Indian go out armed for war. We saw him reconoitre, make signs to his comrades, sleep, warm himself, load his rifle, sharpen his scalping-knife, steal through the grass within rife-shot of his foes, fire, scalp one of them, and dance, whooping, and triumphing. There was a dreadful truth about the whole, and it made our blood run cold.[18]

In the years following their return to Chicago, John and Juliette continued to see their family grow. In the summer of 1835, Juliette gave birth to Eleanor Lytle, or "Nellie," as she came to be called. Nellie was followed two years later by a brother, John Harris Jr. Tragedy struck in 1839, when the family lost their oldest son, six-year-old Alexander Wolcott, the child who had been born at the portage. He had been playing nearby in an empty house with friends when he found a bottle containing corrosive sublimate, a chemical often used as a wood preservative or pesticide. Not knowing any better, the boy took a drink. The loss of their son was so painful for John and Juliette that the boy is not even mentioned in *Wau-Bun*.

It would be four years before another child came into the family. A son, Arthur, was born in 1841. Two years later, Julian Magill was born, but he survived for only six weeks. The couple had two more children, Francis William in 1844 and George Herbert in 1846. Unfortunately, tragedy would continue to follow the Kinzies, when two-year-old Francis was seriously scalded after falling into a tub of boiling water. It was thanks only to Juliette's dogged determination that he survived that accident, yet he succumbed to cholera in 1850 at the age of six. Of their seven children, only three would outlive their parents.

In 1861, when the Civil War broke out between the North and South, the Kinzie family signed up to do their part, as did many other families in Chicago. George, the youngest son, was seventeen and signed up for a one-hundred-day enlistment as a private in the 134th Illinois Volunteer Infantry. By 1863 George, now a second lieutenant, was serving alongside his older brother Arthur, who had attained the rank of captain. Together they were aides-de-camp on the staff of their uncle General David Hunter during his siege against Fort Pulaski near Savannah, Georgia. By 1864, both Kinzie sons had transferred to the staff of General C. C. Washburn, where they had the misfortune of being on duty in Memphis when Nathan Bedford Forrest raided the city. Forrest's aim was to capture several union generals and to release prisoners held in a nearby camp. Washburn escaped in his night shirt but members of his staff, including the two Kinzie brothers, were captured.

The brothers were sent to the prisoner-of-war camp at Cahawba, Alabama. A month later, their sister Nellie, now living in Savannah, Georgia, and married to a Confederate officer, wrote to Jefferson Davis and appealed to his old association with her parents from their days at Fort Winnebago. Nellie implored Davis to use his position as president of the Confederate States of America to release her brothers. Although it had been thirty years since his days as a young lieutenant at Fort Winnebago, Davis remembered the Kinzies—especially John, "whose moral character was above reproach"—and he ordered George and Arthur's release.[19]

Unfortunately, John Harris Jr. wasn't as lucky. The younger Kinzie enlisted in the navy and eventually was promoted to the rank of third master. He was stationed aboard the Mississippi River ironclad steamboat *Mound City.* He was at his post during the battle of Saint Charles on June 17, 1862, when a shot penetrated the ship's steam drum, scalding and killing most of her crew, including John Harris Jr.[20]

As did his three sons, John Kinzie served in the Civil War, but in a role less hazardous than those his sons endured. Kinzie's expertise in financial matters earned him an appointment by President Lincoln as a paymaster with the rank of major in 1861. Overseeing paymaster activities for Michigan, Wisconsin, and Illinois, with only a single clerk to assist him, Kinzie had a severe workload. Though he was able to keep pace with his duties, the strain was telling, but Kinzie refused to ask for help.

After four years, Kinzie finally requested a leave of absence for a much-needed vacation away. His condition was more serious than anyone thought. Fluid was building around his lungs, a condition known at the time as "dropsy of the chest."[21] On the train ride east, he unexpectedly collapsed, as Juliette remembered:

> He set out with his family upon a journey, in hopes that mountain air or sea-bathing would recruit his exhausted forces. But he was des-

Major John H. Kinzie, dressed in his Civil War Paymaster's uniform. NATIONAL ARCHIVES

tined to reach hardly the first stage of his journey. While riding in the cars approaching Pittsburgh, and conversing with his ordinary cheerfulness, he remarked a blind man approaching, and perceiving that he was asking alms, he characteristically put his hand in his pocket. In the act, his head drooped gently, and with a peaceful sigh, his spirit departed to his rest.[22]

Kinzie's body was taken home, where funeral services were held at St. James Church, and he was laid to rest at Graceland Cemetery in Chicago.

12

REMEMBERING JOHN KINZIE

John H. Kinzie was subagent at the portage for four years and seven months. During that period, he took at least four trips that kept him away from the agency for significant stretches of time. His limited tenure in office, coupled with the fact that none of his private papers (those not included in his official Indian Agency correspondence) have survived, make it difficult to judge his impact on the agency or the tribes that surrounded it. There are, however, a number of generalizations that we can make about him.

Kinzie was an efficient public servant who rarely gave his superiors reason to complain about his service. He rarely had problems in settling his financial accounts with the Indian Office; and when problems arose, he was always vindicated. He ensured that annuity payments were made, vaccinations administered, creditors properly dealt with, and treaty obligations fully explained. He was intelligent. Anyone who received the approval of such an exacting boss as Robert Stuart, let alone mastered six Native languages, could not be a slouch. Kinzie took his responsibility as subagent seriously and did the best he could for the Indians under his jurisdiction. His efforts led to the appointment of a doctor for the tribe, and he worked hard to alleviate their suffering during the harsh winter of 1832–33.

Anecdotal stories of Kinzie reveal an affable and often self-effacing personality. Except for his relations with other agents, who themselves were often full of their own hubris, Kinzie got along with nearly everyone who knew him. He enjoyed good relations with the officers of Fort Winnebago, as well as his superiors both in the American Fur Company and in the Office of Indian Affairs.

But Kinzie was also a product of his time and place. Whereas it's true he got along with his superiors, he also never openly challenged them. Nowhere in the surviving correspondence is he critical of the American Fur Company or Cass's association with it. Likewise, though he did all he could to ease the pain of the Ho-Chunk's removal, he rarely if ever challenged the policy itself.

Kinzie remains a part of the collective memory of Wisconsin history thanks to Juliette's writings. Her classic narrative *Wau-Bun* was a successful book when it was first published in 1856 and has since been reprinted at least eleven times. The book remains an often-cited resource for early-nineteenth-century life on the Wisconsin frontier.

But *Wau-Bun* is only one reminder of Kinzie's time in Wisconsin. The agency house still stands, preserved as a museum outside of the city of Portage. Here one can walk the halls and peer into the rooms Kinzie built in the summer of 1832. Following the closure of the agency in 1845, the house remained federal property until 1854, when it was sold into private ownership. By the time of the Civil War, the house had become a farm and would remain so for the next seventy years. By 1920, the building had fallen

The Indian Agency House circa 1930, just prior to restoration by the Colonial Dames.
WHI IMAGE ID 42805

into serious disrepair, but the original floor plan and much of its original characteristics remained. In 1929 local residents developed an interest in the house. With the support of the eminent Wisconsin historian Louise Phelps Kellogg, residents formed an association to preserve the site.[1]

They appealed to the Wisconsin Chapter of The National Society of The Colonial Dames of America for help in the preservation effort. A special reprinting of *Wau-Bun* and Kellogg's article about the agency house published in the *Wisconsin Magazine of History* attracted public attention to the site's preservation. By October 1930 the Wisconsin chapter of the Colonial Dames had raised enough money to purchase the house. An extensive renovation followed. After two years of restoration and one hundred years after its initial construction, the agency house opened as a museum.[2]

For more than eighty years the Colonial Dames have ensured the preservation of the house. Site visits by archaeologists, including a dig around the house in 1988, have provided additional context to the history of the house and its surroundings. In 2010 the house underwent an extensive renovation, and the foundation, siding, chimneys, windows, roof, shutters, and porches were all replaced or restored.[3]

The Indian Agency House today. COURTESY OF DELLA NOHL

The efforts of the Colonial Dames have preserved one of the few tangible relics of early federal Indian policy. Other agencies throughout the country no longer exist or have been moved to new locations. The agencies of Street, Taliaferro, Stambaugh, Wolcott, and others have long since vanished. Schoolcraft's house still stands, but it is no longer on its original foundation.

—‖—

Perhaps the best way to remember Kinzie is not through literary works or museum exhibits, but rather through a recognition that his life story is a useful means by which to study the broader events of his period. A study of Kinzie's life is also the story of the Ho-Chunk Nation during a period of increasing attacks on its cultural existence and its very sovereignty. Kinzie oversaw Ho-Chunk relations during a turbulent time, as the tribe made one futile attempt after another to stem the tide of white advancement on their lands. Coinciding with the construction of Fort Winnebago and the Rock River subagency, Kinzie's subagency marked an increased level of scrutiny and control over the Ho-Chunk. Before 1827 the tribe had one principal Indian agent living on the periphery of their territory, and the only military fort in their region had been removed. After Red Bird's actions, the Ho-Chunk had two army garrisons and three agencies watching over them. In the same time span, the Ho-Chunk saw their land holdings slashed by breathtaking amounts.

In 1837, four years after Kinzie left the portage, the Ho-Chunk ceded all of their remaining lands in Wisconsin to the United States. The subsequent removal effort, which lasted forty years, resulted in a split in the Nation. After 1875, two bands of Ho-Chunk emerged: those who remained on their new lands in the west (now known as the Winnebago Tribe of Nebraska), and the scattered pockets of tribal members who drifted back to Wisconsin. The Wisconsin Ho-Chunk eventually became an Indian nation recognized by the federal government in 1963.

By the turn of the twenty-first century, the Ho-Chunk Nation had established a clear policy to reacquire as much of their traditional lands across Wisconsin as possible. In 2001, the Nation acquired more than 1,200 acres in Richland County along the Kickapoo River, from the defunct

La Farge Dam Project. And by 2003, the Nation had acquired 1,326 acres of former Indian lands in Clark, Jackson, Adams, and Juneau counties.[4]

This land acquisition process has not been without difficulties. For example, a longstanding dispute has arisen between the Nation and Sauk County over the taxation of tribal land. Ho-Chunk lands fall into either of two categories: lands held in trust for the Nation by the Bureau of Indian Affairs, and lands that are not. Lands held in trust are not taxable or subject to ordinances from local governments. Just north of Baraboo, in northeastern Sauk County, the Ho-Chunk operate one of the largest casinos in Wisconsin. Surrounding the casino are 724 acres of land owned by the Nation but not held in trust. In 1996 the Ho-Chunk applied for trust status for these land holdings, which included the casino as well as a wellness center. The amount of acreage to be placed into trust alarmed local officials, who worried about the impact the move would have on the county's tax base.[5]

The County Board of Supervisors voted to oppose the transfer of Ho-Chunk lands.[6] In 1996 and again in 1997, the board passed a resolution opposing any transfer of tribal lands into trust status. The Nation reduced the size of their request to five acres near the casino, but even that was too much for county officials, who feared it was a ploy to set a precedent for future parcels to be placed in trust status.[7] Since then, the county has consistently sought legal means to oppose the Ho-Chunk Nation's submitting arguments to the Bureau of Indian Affairs regarding federal laws on trust lands; in March 2005, the county sought injunctions on lands the bureau approved for trust status.[8]

In 1998 the disposal of Wisconsin's decommissioned Badger Army Ammunition Plant offered yet another opportunity for the Ho-Chunk to rebuild their former territory. Originally built at the onset World War II, the massive munitions facility near Baraboo, Wisconsin, produced artillery and bullet propellant for the Korean War and Vietnam. Within months of the announcement of the plant's decommissioning, the Ho-Chunk Nation requested transfer of 3,000 acres of land at the plant. Their request comprised almost half of the land available, and the political realities of such a sizeable request led the Nation to scale back its claim to 1,500 acres. The Ho-Chunk cited three reasons for acquiring the land: expansion of a bison herd project, reacquisition of traditional lands, and preservation of cultural resources. After sixteen years of negotiations and several occasions where land transfers seemed impossible, US Senator Tammy Baldwin announced in December 2014 that 1,553 acres would be transferred to the Nation. Six months later, on June 26, 2015, nearly three hundred spectators, including Ho-Chunks, area residents, and local, state, and federal officials, gathered at the old munitions plant and celebrated the end of a seventeen-year struggle to reclaim a portion of their homeland.[9]

The Ho-Chunk Nation has endured. The struggles to rebuild tribal lands serve as the most tangible illustration that 180 years after John H. Kinzie left the Fort Winnebago subagency, the federal policies that he represented still affect life in Wisconsin and will continue to do so as long as the Ho-Chunk remain.

—⊣⊢—

Studying the life of John H. Kinzie is a challenging exercise. It is a shame that we have so little evidence of his point of view. If only we had his journal; if only his letters to and from Juliette had survived the Chicago fire of 1871. What details would they have contained?

Wau-Bun was first published in 1856, nine years before Kinzie's death. We can presume that he read and approved of Juliette's narrative, so we may equally presume that the narrative in some manner reflects his perspective. In the official correspondence of the Office of Indian Affairs we get a glimpse of what Kinzie thought of Joseph Street and Samuel Stambaugh, but there had to be more. Did he ever get angry? Did he have an ego? Was there more to his relationship with Lewis Cass? What was his impression of Four Legs or other leaders of the Ho-Chunk Nation?

But the lack of his personal papers does not prevent us from understanding life in early nineteenth-century Wisconsin. There are plenty of records, both official and private, including those of other Indian agents, that still exist. But the lack of John Kinzie's papers deprives us of an opportunity to view the nineteenth century from a unique perspective, that of a man who was a product of the Great Lakes frontier, of a man who—if Harriet Martineau was right—was one of the few white people to speak of Native Americans with any regard. Given the events Kinzie witnessed and the people he knew, one cannot help wondering: What would he have said?

Notes

Introduction

1. J. H. Mullett, exterior field notes, township 13 north, range 9 east, Wisconsin Public Land Survey Records, Wisconsin Board of Commissioners of Public Lands (October 1831).
2. For a detailed synopsis of Wisconsin during this period see Lucy Eldersveld Murphy, *A Gathering of Rivers Indians, Métis, and Mining in the Western Great Lakes, 1737–1832* (Lincoln: University of Nebraska Press, 2000).
3. For a good overview of the experience of mixed-ancestry inhabitants and their troubles after the War of 1812, see John D. Haeger, "A Time of Change: Green Bay, 1815–1834," *Wisconsin Magazine of History* 54, no. 4 (Summer 1971), 285–298.

Chapter 1

1. Juliette Kinzie, *Wau-Bun: The "Early Day" in the North-West* (Urbana: University of Illinois Press, 1992), 79.
2. Kinzie, *Wau-Bun*, 1992 edition, 66.
3. Kinzie, *Wau-Bun*, 1992 edition, 80.
4. John Kinzie to Secretary of War, December 5, 1830, US Government National Archives Microfilm Publications Microcopy 234, *Letters Received by the Office of Indian Affairs 1884–1881, R931, Winnebago Agency, 1826–1875* (Washington, DC: National Archives Microfilm Publications, 1956), hereafter referred to as M234 R931.
5. Ibid.
6. William Hamilton to John Kinzie, November 14, 1830, M234 R931.
7. Ibid.
8. Kinzie to Secretary of War, December 5, 1830, M234 R931.
9. Ibid.
10. An extensive compilation of laws and treaties for this period can be found in United States and Samuel S. Hamilton, *Indian Treaties, and Laws and Regulations Relating to Indian Affairs to Which Is Added an Appendix, Containing*

the *Proceedings of the Old Congress, and Other Important State Papers, in Relation to Indian Affairs* (Washington City: Way & Gideon, printers, 1826).

11. For a complete overview of American Indian policy during this period and the role of the Trade and Intercourse Act of 1802, see Francis Paul Prucha, *American Indian Policy in the Formative Years: The Trade and Intercourse Acts 1790–1834* (Cambridge, MA: Harvard University Press, 1962). For a copy of the act see Francis Paul Prucha, ed., *Documents of United States Indian Policy,* 2nd ed. (Lincoln: University of Nebraska Press, 1990).

12. Ulrich Danckers, Jane Meredith, John F. Swenson, and Helen Hornbeck Tanner, *A Compendium of the Early History of Chicago: To the Year 1835 when the Indians Left* (River Forest, IL: Early Chicago, 2000), 217.

Chapter 2

1. Detailed biographical and genealogical information on John Kinzie Sr. and the Kinzie family can be found in Ann Durkin Keating, *Rising Up from Indian Country: The Battle of Fort Dearborn and the Birth of Chicago* (Chicago: University of Chicago Press, 2012), and Ulrich Danckers, Jane Meredith, John F. Swenson, and Helen Hornbeck Tanner, *A Compendium of the Early History of Chicago: To the Year 1835 when the Indians Left* (River Forest, IL: Early Chicago, 2000).

2. Keating, *Rising Up,* 26–27, 43; Danckers et al., *Early Chicago,* 226.

3. Keating, *Rising Up,* 36–38.

4. Ibid., 63.

5. Gurdon Saltonstall Hubbard and Henry E. Hamilton, *Incidents and Events in the Life of Gurdon Saltonstall Hubbard* (Chicago: Rand, McNally & Co., 1888), 27.

6. Keating, *Rising Up,* 117–119; Danckers et al., *Early Chicago,* 221.

7. Danckers et al., *Early Chicago,* 155.

8. Keating, *Rising Up,* 142

9. Juliette Kinzie, *Wau-Bun: The "Early Day" in the North-West* (Urbana: University of Illinois Press, 1992), 125.

10. Keating, *Rising Up,* 156–157.

11. Danckers et al., *Early Chicago,* 147.

12. Juliette Kinzie, "Sketch of the Late Col. John H. Kinzie," *Addresses Delivered at the Annual Meeting of the Chicago Historical Society, November 29, 1868,* Fergus' Historical Series, vol. 20, 1877, 22.

13. Ibid.

14. Silas Farmer, *The History of Detroit and Michigan* (Detroit, MI: Silas Farmer and Co., 1889), 715.

15. An excellent overview of Astor's career and the development of the American Fur Company can be found in John Upton Terrell, *Furs by Astor* (New York: William Morrow & Co., 1963).

16. Hubbard and Hamilton, *Incidents and Events*, 26–27.

17. Ibid., 19.

18. Kinzie, "Sketch," 23; Theodore C. Blegen, ed., *The Unfinished Autobiography of Henry Hastings Sibley Together with a Selection of Hitherto Unpublished Letters from the Thirties* (Minneapolis: The Voyageur Press, 1932), 16–18.

19. Hubbard and Hamilton, *Incidents and Events*, 70.

20. Ibid., 71.

21. Ibid., 117, 134.

22. Rodney B. Nelson, *Beaumont, America's First Physiologist* (Geneva, IL: Grant House Press, 1990), 106.

Chapter 3

1. James Lockwood, "Early Times and Events in Wisconsin," *Collections of the State Historical Society of Wisconsin*, vol. 2 (Madison: State Historical Society of Wisconsin, 1856), 173–174. Kinzie's name can also be found on several petitions during this period, suggesting a rise in his social stature; see Clarence E. Carter, ed., *The Territorial Papers of the United States, vol. 11: The Territory of Michigan, 1820–1829* (Washington, DC: United States Government Printing Office, 1943), 482, 593, 819.

2. Juliette Kinzie, "Sketch of the Late Col. John H. Kinzie," *Addresses Delivered at the Annual Meeting of the Chicago Historical Society, November 29, 1868*, Fergus' Historical Series, vol. 20, 1877; "Field Notes for John Harris Kinzie and Juliette Magill Kinzie," Federal Writers' Project (Wis.), Writings and Research Notes, 1935–1942, Wis Mss MM, Box 24, Wisconsin Historical Society Archives. Juliette confirms Kinzie's knowledge of Ojibwe in Juliette Kinzie, *Wau-Bun: The "Early Day" in the North-West* (Urbana: University of Illinois Press, 1992), 26. A copy of the Winnebago dictionary is on file at the Chicago Historical Society.

3. Lockwood, "Early Times and Events," 168–169.

4. Fergus' *Directory of the City of Chicago, 1839*, part 128; Kinzie, *Wau-Bun*, 63–66.

5. Bruce E. Mahan, *Old Fort Crawford and the Frontier* (Prairie du Chien, WI: Prairie du Chien Historical Society, 2000), p. 93. A through overview of the Treaty of 1825 at Prairie du Chien can be found in Charles A. Abele, "The Grand Indian Council and Treaty at Prairie du Chien, 1825," (PhD diss., Loyola University, 1969).

6. Lewis Cass, "British Indian Policy in Respect to the Indians (January 1840)," *North American Review* 258, no. 4, Special Heritage Issue: The Indian Question, 1823–1973 (Winter 1973).

7. British Indian policy following the War of 1812 is covered extensively in Colin G. Calloway, "The End of an Era: British-Indian Relations in the Great Lakes Region after the War of 1812," *Michigan Historical Review* 12, no. 2 (Fall 1986): 1–20.

8. John Upton Terrell, *Furs by Astor* (New York: William Morrow & Co., 1963), 137–139.

9. Joseph Schafer, *The Wisconsin Lead Region* (Madison: State Historical Society of Wisconsin, 1932), 21.

10. Ibid., 23.

11. Charles J. Kappler, *Indian Affairs Laws and Treaties*, vol. 2 (Treaties 1778–1883) (Washington: Government Printing Office, 1904), 132–133; Reuben Gold Thwaites, "Notes on Early Lead Mining in the Fever (or Galena) River Region," *Collections of the State Historical Society of Wisconsin*, vol. 13 (Madison: State Historical Society of Wisconsin, 1895), 286–287.

12. James A. Wilgus, "The Century Old Lead Region in Early Wisconsin History," *Wisconsin Magazine of History* 10, no. 4 (June 1927): 402; Thwaites, "Notes on Early Lead Mining," 289–290.

13. Schafer, *The Wisconsin Lead Region*, 12.

14. Ibid., 36.

15. Schafer in *The Wisconsin Lead Region* states that lead production increased dramatically in the late 1820s. In 1826, 856,000 pounds of lead were produced at the Fever River Mines. In 1827 the number grew to 5,182,180 pounds. In 1828, 11,105,810 pounds of lead were taken out of the ground.

16. Carter, *Territorial Papers, vol. 11*, 24.

17. Francis Paul Prucha, *Broad Axe and Bayonet: The Role of the United States Army in the Development of the Northwest, 1815–1860* (Lincoln: University of Nebraska Press, 1953), 85–86.

18. Jedediah Morse, *A Report of the Secretary of War of the United States on Indian Affairs* (New Haven, CT: S. Converse, 1822), 48; Lyman C. Draper, ed., "The Fur Trade and Factory System at Green Bay 1816–1821," *Report and Collections of the State Historical Society of Wisconsin*, vol. 7 (Madison: State Historical Society of Wisconsin, 1876), 278–288.

19. Morse, *A Report of the Secretary of War of the United States on Indian Affairs*, 48.

20. Mahan, *Old Fort Crawford*, 93.

21. "Journal of the Commissioners Appointed to Treat with the Indians Assembled at Prairie du Chien in July and August 1825," found in US Government National Archives Microfilm Publications Microcopy T494, United States Bureau of Indian Affairs, Documents Relating to the Negotiation of Ratified and Unratified Treaties with the Various Tribes of Indians, 1801–69, R2, Ratified Treaty No. 139, Documents Relating to the Negotiation of the Treaty of August 19, 1825, with the Sioux, Chippewa, Sauk and Fox, Menominee, Iowa and Winnebago Indians and Part of the Ottawa, Chippewa, and Potawatomi of the Illinois Indians, 38–39.

22. Kinzie, *Wau-Bun*, 1992 edition, 42–45.

23. Ibid., 42–45.

24. John Johnston and Charlotte Reeve Conover, *Recollections of 60 Years on the Ohio Frontier* (Van Buren, OH: R. E. Davis, 2001), 70.

25. John Gilmary Shea Papers, box 8, folder 11, Georgetown University. Kinzie's eight-page report is on file at the Chicago Historical Society.

26. The location of the council grounds is on the west bank of Little Lake Butte des Morts just north of Fritse Park. Daughters of the American Revolution, "Report of the Old Trails Committee," 1920, SC 2374; Charles V. Donaldson, "Little Buttes des Morts, and Its Former Appearances, 1905," SC 2368, both papers on file at the Wisconsin Historical Society Archives; A. G. Ellis, 1834 Public Land Survey, sketch map for T20N R17E, Wisconsin Board of Commissioners of Public Lands.

Chapter 4

1. Louise Phelps Kellogg, *The British Régime in Wisconsin and the Northwest* (Madison: State Historical Society of Wisconsin, 1935), 155–157.

2. Richard White, *The Middle Ground: Indians, Empires, and Republics in the Great Lakes Region, 1650–1815* (Cambridge: Cambridge University Press, 1991), 511.

3. The Wisconsin Cartographer's Guild, *Wisconsin's Past and Present: A Historical Atlas* (Madison: University of Wisconsin Press, 1998), 9.

4. Jeanne Kay, "The Fur Trade and Native American Population Growth," *Ethnohistory* 31, no. 4 (Autumn 1984): 282.

5. "Papers of Capt. T. G. Anderson, British Indian Agent," *Collections of the State Historical Society of Wisconsin*, vol. 10 (Madison: State Historical Society of Wisconsin, 1888), 143; see also Mark Diedrich, *Ho-Chunk Chiefs: Winnebago Leadership in an Era of Crisis* (Rochester, MN: Coyote Books, 2001), 48–50.

6. J. A. Jones and Alice E. Smith, *Winnebago Indians: Winnebago Ethnology* (New York: Garland, 1974), 134.

7. Jones and Smith, *Winnebago Indians*, 135; Mark Diedrich, *Ho-Chunk Chiefs*, 26; Letter from the Secretary of War in Relation to the Hostile Disposition of Indian Tribes on the Northwestern Frontier, 20th Cong., 1st sess., House Document no. 277, serial 175, 9.

8. John D. Morris, *Sword of the Border: Major General Jacob Jennings Brown, 1775–1828* (Kent, OH: Kent State University Press, 2000), 238.

9. James Lockwood, "Early Times and Events in Wisconsin," *Collections of the State Historical Society of Wisconsin*, vol. 2 (Madison: State Historical Society of Wisconsin, 1856), 156; Indictments and transcripts relating to the Methode murder trial, County of Crawford Circuit Court Term of May 1827, found in US Government National Archives Microfilm Publications M234, *Letters Received by the Office of Indian Affairs 1824–1881, R931, Winnebago Agency, 1826–1875* (Washington, DC: National Archives Microfilm Publications, 1956), hereafter referred to as M234 R931.

10. Indictments and transcripts of the Methode murder trial, M234 R931, 11; Colonel W. Morgan to Acting Assistant Adjutant General Butler, July 9, 1826, M234 R931.

12. Ibid.

13. Ibid.

14. Ibid.

15. Ibid.

16. Peter L. Scanlan, "Nicolas Boilvin, Indian Agent," *Wisconsin Magazine of History* 27, no. 2 (December 1943), 168.

17. William J. Snelling, "Early Days at Prairie du Chien and the Winnebago Outbreak of 1827," *Collections of the State Historical Society of Wisconsin,* vol. 5 (Madison: State Historical Society of Wisconsin, 1907), 132–135; Barbara K. Luecke and John C. Snelling, *Minnesota's First Family* (Eagan, MN: Grenadier, 1993), 177–178; Carter, *Territorial Papers Vol. 11,* 1082.

18. Ninian W. Edwards, *History of Illinois, from 1778 to 1833 and Life and Times of Ninian Edwards* (Springfield: Illinois State Journal, 1870), 219; Joseph Street to Secretary of War, November 15, 1827, US Government National Archives Microfilm Publications Microcopy 234 Roll 696, *Letters Received by the Office of Indian Affairs, Prairie du Chien Agency 1824–1833* (Washington, DC: National Archives and Records Service General Services Administration, 1957), hereafter referred to as M234 R696; Diedrich, *Ho-Chunk Chiefs,* 71.

19. Snelling, "Early Days," 143–144; Edwards, *History of Illinois,* 219; Lawrence Taliaferro to William Clark, August 1, 1827, and Lawrence Taliaferro to Colonel J. Snelling, August 1, 1827, both in Helen M. White, ed., *Lawrence Taliaferro Papers 1813–1868* (St. Paul: Minnesota Historical Society, 1965).

20. A letter written by John Marsh to William Clark (M234 R748) reported that a joint Ho-Chunk and Dakota war party had set out against the Ojibwe on May 28. The party was led by the Dakota leader L'Arc. It is possible that this was the war party that Red Bird participated in. L'Arc would later warn Marsh about Ho-Chunk plans for attacking Americans in the Upper Mississippi Valley.

21. Snelling, "Early Days," 143; Thomas L. McKenney, "The Winnebago War," *Collections of the State Historical Society of Wisconsin,* vol. 5 (Madison: State Historical Society of Wisconsin, 1907), 201.

22. "Journal of the Proceedings of the Council Held with the Winnebago Indians at Green Bay by Governor Cass and Colonel Menard, Commissioners," entry for August 21, found in US Government National Archives Microfilm Publications Microcopy no. T 494, United States Bureau of Indian Affairs, Documents Relating to the Negotiation of Ratified and Unratified Treaties with the Various Tribes of Indians, 1801–69, R2, Ratified Treaty

no. 153, Documents Relating to the Negotiation of the Treaty of August 25, 1828, with the Winnebago and United Potowatomie, Chippewa, and Ottowa Indians.

23. Martin Zanger, "Red Bird," *American Indian Leaders: Studies in Diversity,* edited by R. David Edmunds (Lincoln: University of Nebraska Press, 1981), 70; McKenney, "The Winnebago War," 201.

24. Edwards, *History of Illinois,* 291; Snelling, "Early Days," 144.

25. William R. Smith, *The History of Wisconsin: In Three Parts, Historical Documentary, and Descriptive,* vol. 3 (Madison: Beriah Brown, 1854), 349; Lockwood, "Early Times and Events," 161.

26. There is no marker noting the location of Gagnier's home. Prairie du Chien historian Peter Scanlan had successfully located the site in the 1920s, with plans for the erection of a marker, but for reasons unknown he was never able to follow through with his plans. The location can be found along the east side of Highway 18 just south of Prairie du Chien, not far from the city's airport. Today a Walmart stands atop or just adjacent to the site. Robert Marzim, "Note on Phase One Testing at the Gagnier Site: Prairie du Chien, Wisconsin," (unpublished manuscript, 2000, on file at Sangamo Archeological Center); "Massacre Scene Found Near Sugar Loaf Hill," *Wisconsin State Journal,* June 30, 1935 (Wisconsin Historical Society Archives); Peter L. Scanlan, *Prairie du Chien: French, British, American* (Prairie du Chien, WI: Prairie du Chien Historical Society, 1998), 130.

27. Letter of Mrs. John B. Ducharme, 1905, SC 2572, WHS Archives.

28. An excellent map of Prairie du Chien circa 1828 is on file at the Wisconsin Historical Society Archives. The map notes lot 43 as owned by Thomas McNair. The map also notes two cabins just across the eastern boundary line of McNair's lot at the entrance of McNair's Coulee. See "Plat of Private Claims at Prairie du Chien, WI," WHS Image ID 53101, WHS Archives; Marzim, "Note on Phase One Testing."

29. Snelling, "Early Days," 146; Lockwood, "Early Times and Events," 161; Smith, *History of Wisconsin,* 350; Zanger, *American Indian Leaders,* 71; Letter of Mrs. John B. Ducharme, 1905; "Trials and Decisions of the Several Courts Held in the Counties Michilimackinac, Brown and Crawford, 1823–1830," found in Wis Mss DD, James Duane Doty Papers, 1779–1879, WHS Archives. A number of differing accounts of this attack exist. There are three versions of Theresa Gagnier's testimony alone. The most accurate

record probably can be found in Doty's "Trials and Decisions," which also includes a brief statement by Pascal Menard and the trial testimony of Red Bird's son. All differ in many respects. The narrative provided here is a composite of the accounts.

30. Smith, *History of Wisconsin*, 350.

31. Lockwood, "Early Times and Events," 162.

32. Clarence E. Carter, ed., *The Territorial Papers of the United States, vol. 11: The Territory of Michigan, 1820–1829* (Washington, DC: United States Government Printing Office, 1943), 1096; George D. Lyman, *John Marsh, Pioneer; The Life Story of a Trail-Blazer on Six Frontiers* (New York: C. Scribner's Sons, 1935), 123.

33. Lawrence Taliaferro to William Clark, August 8, 1827, US Government National Archives Microfilm Publications Microcopy 234, *Letters Received by the Office of Indian Affairs, 1824–1881, Roll 757, St. Peter's Agency 1824–1836* (Washington, DC: National Archives Microfilm Publications, 1956), hereafter referred to as M234 R757.

34. John Marsh to William Clark, July 20, 1827 M234 R 748.

35. "Report of the Commissioners Cass & McKenney with the Treaty Made by Them with the Indians at the Butte des Morts in 1827," Ratified Treaty no. 148, Document Relating to the Treaty of 1827, US Government National Archives Microfilm Publications Microcopy T494, United States Bureau of Indian Affairs. Documents Relating to the Negotiation of Ratified and Unratified Treaties with Various Tribes of Indians, 1801–1869 (Washington, DC: National Archives Microfilm Publications, 1960).

36. Ibid., 22.

37. Ibid., entire journal.

38. Ibid., 23.

39. Ibid., 28.

40. Ibid.

41. Thomas L. McKenney, *Memoirs Official and Personal* (Lincoln: University of Nebraska Press, 1973), 99–103.

42. Ibid., 179.

43. McKenney, "The Winnebago War," 180.

44. Juliette Kinzie, "Sketch of the Late Col. John H. Kinzie," *Addresses Delivered at the Annual Meeting of the Chicago Historical Society, November 29, 1868,* Fergus' Historical Series, vol. 20, 1877.

45. John Kinzie to E. A. Brush, September 4, 1827, Letters, 1827–1832, File 1827, WHS Archives.

46. McKenney, "The Winnebago War," 182.

47. Ibid., 186.

48. Roger L. Nichols, *General Henry Atkinson: A Western Military Career* (Norman: University of Oklahoma Press, 1965), 133; General Henry Atkinson to General Edmund Gaines, 20th Cong. 1st Session, doc. no. 2, 157.

49. Atkinson to Gaines, 20th Cong. 1st Sess., doc. no 2, 157.

50. Letter from the Secretary of War in Relation to the Hostile Disposition of Indian Tribes on the Northwestern Frontier, *Congressional Serial Set no. 175*, 20th Cong., 1st Sess., House doc. no. 277 (Washington, DC: Gales and Seaton, 1828), 17, hereafter referred to as *Congressional Serial Set 175*.

Chapter 5

1. Letter from the Secretary of War in Relation to the Hostile Disposition of Indian Tribes on the Northwestern Frontier, *Congressional Serial Set no. 175*, 18.

2. Atkinson's provisional treaty, *Congressional Serial Set no. 169*, 20th Cong., 1st Sess., House doc. no. 2, Item M, (Washington, DC: Gales and Seaton, 1828), 153.

3. John Connelly to William Clark, February 12, 1828, M234 R696.

4. Thomas McKenney to the Secretary of War, January 24, 1828, M234 R931.

5. Ibid.

6. Ibid.; Louise P. Kellogg, "The Winnebago Visit to Washington in 1828," *Transactions of the Wisconsin Academy of Sciences, Arts, and Letters 39* (1935): 349.

7. Juliette Kinzie, *Wau-Bun: The "Early Day" in the North-West* (Urbana: University of Illinois Press, 1992), 48.

8. Report of General Macomb, General of the Army, *Congressional Serial Set no. 181*, 20th Cong., 2nd Sess., Senate documents, (Washington, DC: Gales and Seaton, 1828), 17–18, hereafter referred to as *Congressional Serial Set 181*, Macomb's Report.

9. Documents from the War Department, Accompanying the President's Message to Congress. *Congressional Serial Set. no. 169*, 20th Cong., 1st Sess., Senate documents, Document A, (Washington, DC: Gales and Seaton, 1828), 49.

10. *Congressional Serial Set 181*, Macomb's Report, 26.

11. William Clark to the Secretary of War, July 10, 1828, M234 R748.

12. Thomas Forsyth to William Clark, June 25, 1828, M234 R748.

13. John Connolly to Thomas Forsyth, June 23, 1828, M234 R748.

14. Ibid.

15. Ibid., entry for August 21, 1828.

16. For the exact description of the boundary line see Treaty of 1828, Article 1 found in Charles J. Kappler, *Indian Affairs Laws and Treaties*, vol. 2, Treaties 1778–1883 (Washington: Government Printing Office, 1904), 292.

17. Ibid., 292–294.

18. Andrew Jackson Turner, "The History of Fort Winnebago," *Collections of the State Historical Society of Wisconsin*, vol. 14 (Madison: State Historical Society of Wisconsin, 1898), 71.

19. Ibid., 72.

20. Lieutenant J. F. Davis to Major General Jesup, June 1, 1831, found in Jefferson Davis, *The Papers of Jefferson Davis*, vol. 1 (Baton Rouge: Louisiana State University Press, 1971), 199–200.

21. Francis B. Heitman, *Historical Register and Dictionary of the United States Army, from its Organization, September 29, 1789, to March 2, 1903*, vol. 1. (Urbana: University of Illinois Press, 1965), 430; Ulrich Danckers, Jane Meredith, John F. Swenson, and Helen Hornbeck Tanner, *A Compendium of the Early History of Chicago: To the Year 1835 when the Indians Left* (River Forest, IL: Early Chicago, 2000), 147.

22. Mark Diedrich, *Ho-Chunk Chiefs: Winnebago Leadership in an Era of Crisis* (Rochester, MN: Coyote Books, 2001), 28; Herman J. Viola, *Diplomats in Buckskins: A History of Indian Delegations in Washington City* (Bluffton, SC: Rivilo Books, 1995), 97; Kellogg, "The Winnebago Visit," 348, 350.

23. Diedrich, *Ho-Chunk Chiefs*, 28.

24. Kellogg, "The Winnebago Visit," 350; "Abstract of Expenditures on Accounts of the Deputation of Winnebago Indians," M234 R931.

25. *Connecticut Journal* (New Haven), November 4, 1828; *Commercial Advertiser* (New York), October 28, 1828.

26. Kellogg, "The Winnebago Visit," 351–352; *Rhode Island American* (Providence), October 28, 1828, and October 31, 1828; *American Repertory* (St. Albans, Vermont), December 4, 1828.

27. *National Gazette* (Philadephia), October 30, 1828.

28. Ibid.

29. Kellogg, "The Winnebago Visit," 352; Viola, *Diplomats in Buckskin*, 128.

30. Diedrich, *Ho-Chunk Chiefs*, 28; Kellogg, "The Winnebago Visit," 352–353.

31. *Daily National Intelligencer* (Washington, DC), December 6, 1828.

32. Ibid.

33. Ibid.

34. Ibid.

35. Ibid.

36. Ibid.

37. Ibid.

38. Ibid., December 13, 1828.

39. Ibid.

Chapter 6

1. Report from the Secretary of War, in Compliance with Resolutions of the Senate on the 10th of December and 15th of January, Relative to Indian Affairs, &c. &c. 20th Cong. 2nd sess., 1828–1829, Senate document 72, *US Serial Set 181*, 4, 62.

2. Samuel Stambaugh to John Eaton, September 20, 1830, US Government National Archives Microfilm Publications Microcopy 234, *Letters Received by the Office of Indian Affairs, 1824–1881, Roll 315, Green Bay Agency 1824–1832* (Washington, DC: National Archives Microfilm Publications, 1959).

3. House doc. no. 18, (1832), 113, and House doc. no. 101 (1831), 108.

4. David S. Heidler and Jeanie T. Heidler, ed., *Encyclopedia of the War of 1812* (Santa Barbara, CA: Abc-Clio, 1997), 355. McNiel was a brevetted brigadier general for his service in the War of 1812. After the war, however, he remained officially a colonel in command of the First Infantry. Though he is often referred to as "General" McNiel in the correspondence, I have used the title "Colonel," which appears in the official army registers for the time period.

5. Secretary of War to McNiel and Menard, March 30, 1829, Proceedings of the Commissioners for Holding a Treaty with the Winnebagoes and the United Nations of the Ottaways, Chippaways and Potawatomies, entry of June 19, 1829; John Eaton to Caleb Atwater, May 19, 1829, as found in Ratified Treaty no. 155, Documents Relating to the Negotiation of the Treaty of July 29, 1829, with the United Chippewa, Ottawa, and Potawatomi Indi-

ans, MT494 Roll 2, hereafter referred to as Journal of Proceedings, Treaty of 1829, MT494 R2.

6. Kinzie to Cass, June 28, 1829, US Government National Archives Microfilm Publications Microcopy M1, *Records of the Michigan Superintendency of Indian Affairs: Letters Received by the Superintendents, Lewis Cass (1819–1831), George B. Porter (1831–1834), Stevens T. Mason (1834–1835), and John L. Horner (1835) 1829–1835*. 31 vols. (Washington, DC: National Archives Microfilm Publications, 1941), Roll 24, hereafter referred to as M1.

7. Caleb Atwater and Isaac N. Whiting, *Remarks Made on a Tour to Prairie du Chien: Thence to Washington City, in 1829* (Columbus, OH: Isaac N. Whiting, 1831), 3.

8. Atwater and Whiting, *Remarks Made on a Tour*, 54; Secretary of War to McNiel and Menard, March 30, 1829, Journal of Proceedings, Treaty of 1829, MT494 R2.

9. Secretary of War to McNiel and Menard, March 30, 1829, Journal of Proceedings, Treaty of 1829, MT494 R2.

10. Ibid., 68.

11. Caleb Atwater to the Secretary of War, October 28, 1829, M234 R696.

12. Ibid., 68.

13. Journal of Proceedings, Treaty of 1829, MT494 R2, entry of July 18, 1829.

14. Ibid.

15. Atwater and Whiting, *Remarks Made on a Tour*, 70.

16. Ibid., 70.

17. Ibid., 70.

18. Journal of Proceedings, Treaty of 1829, MT494 R2, entry of July 27, 1829.

19. Ibid.

20. Major David Twiggs to Commissioners McNiel and Menard, June 18, 1929, Journal of Proceedings, Treaty of 1829, MT494 R2.

21. Journal of Proceedings, Treaty of 1829, MT494 R2, entry of July 25, 1829.

22. Journal of Proceedings, Treaty of 1829, MT494 R2, entry of July 27, 1829.

23. Charles J. Kappler, *Indian Affairs Laws and Treaties*, vol. 2, Treaties 1778–1883 (Washington: Government Printing Office, 1904), 300–303; Treaty of 1829, Articles 2 and 3. Both treaties also provided numerous land grants to Métis relatives of all the tribes. All of the land grants, however, were to be located outside the mineral country.

24. Joseph Street to Lawrence Taliaferro, August 12, 1829, in Helen M. White,

ed., *Lawrence Taliaferro Papers 1813–1868* (St. Paul: Minnesota Historical Society, 1965), Roll 1, Document 117.

25. Kinzie to Cass, August 6, 1829, M1 R25.

Chapter 7

1. Samuel Stambaugh to John Eaton, September 20, 1830, M234 R315.

2. Ulrich Danckers, Jane Meredith, John F. Swenson, and Helen Hornbeck Tanner, *A Compendium of the Early History of Chicago: To the Year 1835 when the Indians Left* (River Forest, IL: Early Chicago, 2000), 364.

3. Nina Baym, introduction to Juliette Kinzie, *Wau-Bun: The "Early Day" in the North-West* (Urbana: University of Illinois Press, 1992); Louise Phelps Kellogg's introduction can be found in the 1989 edition of *Wau-Bun*: Juliette Kinzie, *Wau-Bun: The "Early Day" in the North-West* (Manasha: Banta Publishing Co., 1989).

4. Kinzie, *Wau-Bun*, 1992 edition, 162.

5. Kinzie, *Wau-Bun*, 1992 edition, 162.

6. Kinzie, *Wau-Bun*, 1989 edition, xvii.

7. Nellie Gordon to Jefferson Davis, September 1, 1864, Museum of the Confederacy.

8. Juliette Kinzie, "Sketch of the Late Col. John H. Kinzie," *Addresses Delivered at the Annual Meeting of the Chicago Historical Society, November 29, 1868*, Fergus' Historical Series, vol. 20, 1877, 26; Danckers et al., *A Compendium*, 225.

9. Kinzie, *Wau-Bun*, 1989 edition, 60.

10. Kinzie to Herring, April 24, 1832, M234 R931.

11. Ibid.

12. Kinzie to Cass, February 16, 1831, found in "Correspondence on the Subject of the Emigration of Indians Between the 30th November, 1831, and 27th December, 1833," Senate doc. 512, vol. 2, 412. Found online at http://memory.loc.gov/ammem/amlaw/lawhome.html, hereafter referred to as Senate doc. 512.

13. Joseph Street to the Secretary of War, August 12, 1829, M234 R696.

14. "Romantic Career was Gen. Street's," *Milwaukee Sentinel*, May 19, 1907; Wisconsin Historical Society, Wisconsin Local History and Biography Articles.

15. This definition of militia was taken from Peter Shrake, "Chasing an Elusive War: The Illinois Militia and the Winnebago War of 1827," *Journal of Illinois History* 12, no. 1 (Spring 2009): 28.

16. Ronald Ryman, "The Role of the Frontier Indian Agent, Joseph Montfort Street, 1827–1840" (master's thesis, Drake University, 1974), 25–26. Letters describing his relationship with Edwards and his lobbying for the Prairie du Chien agency can be found in E. B. Washburne, ed., *The Edwards Papers* (Chicago: Fergus Printing, 1884).

17. John Upton Terrell, *Furs by Astor* (New York: William Morrow & Co., 1963), 251.

18. Ibid., 250–253, 277, 279; for a biographical note on Puthuff, see "The Fur Trade in Wisconsin," *Wisconsin Historical Collections*, vol. 19 (Madison: State Historical Society of Wisconsin, 1910), 407–408.

19. Clarence E. Carter, ed., *The Territorial Papers of the United States, vol. 11: The Territory of Michigan, 1820–1829* (Washington, DC: United States Government Printing Office, 1943), 607.

Chapter 8

1. Much has been written about the origins of the Black Hawk War. For a full treatment of the war and the role of the various tribes involved, see Patrick J. Jung, *The Black Hawk War of 1832* (Norman: University of Oklahoma Press, 2007); and John W. Hall, *Uncommon Defense: Indian Allies in the Black Hawk War* (Cambridge, MA: Harvard University Press, 2009).

2. Atkinson to Kinzie, April 16, 1832, in Ellen M. Whitney, ed., *The Black Hawk War, 1831–1832*, 2 vols. Collections of the Illinois Historical Library, vols. 35–38 (Springfield: Illinois Historical Library, 1970–78), 257–258.

3. Copies of Kinzie's correspondence can be found at M1 R30 and R31.

4. John Kinzie to General Atkinson or Brady, June 7, 1832, in Whitney, *The Black Hawk War*, 542.

5. Jung, *Black Hawk War*, 104.

6. "Narrative of Spoon Decorah," *Collections of the State Historical Society of Wisconsin*, vol. 13 (Madison: State Historical Society of Wisconsin, 1895), 453.

7. Jung, *Black Hawk War*, 78–79.

8. Hall, *Uncommon Defense*, 150.

9. John Kinzie to George B. Porter, July 12, 1832, in Whitney, *Black Hawk War*, 774–775.

10. Kinzie to Porter, Aug 9, 1832, in Whitney, *Black Hawk War*, 974.

11. Juliette Kinzie, *Wau-Bun: The "Early Day" in the North-West* (Urbana: University of Illinois Press, 1992), 231–236.

12. Ibid., 349–350.

13. Street to Atkinson, June 6–7, 1832, in Whitney, *Black Hawk War*, 537.

14. Ibid., 495.

15. Kinzie to Porter, June 11, 1832, M1 R30.

16. Jung, *Black Hawk War*, 104.

17. Atkinson to the Winnebago Indians, in Whitney, *Black Hawk War*, 572.

18. Kinzie to Porter, June 18, 1832, in Whitney, *Black Hawk War*, 626.

Chapter 9

1. Peter L. Scanlan, "Nicolas Boilvin, Indian Agent," *Wisconsin Magazine of History* 27, no. 2 (December 1943): 159; Alice E. Smith, *James Duane Doty: Frontier Promoter* (Madison: State Historical Society of Wisconsin, 1954), 131.

2. Richard G. Bremer, *Indian Agent and Wilderness Scholar: The Life of Henry Rowe Schoolcraft* (Mount Pleasant, MI: Clarke Historical Library, Central Michigan University, 1987), 82–83.

3. Milo Milton Quaife, *Chicago and the Old Northwest, 1673–1835: A Study of the Evolution of the Northwestern Frontier, Together with a History of Fort Dearborn* (Chicago: University of Illinois Press, 2001), 270.

4. Henry H. Hurlbut, *Chicago Antiquities: Comprising Original Items and Relations, Letters, Extracts, and Notes, Pertaining to Early Chicago* (Chicago: For the author, 1881), 105; Quaife, *Chicago and the Old Northwest*, 271.

5. Stambaugh to Eaton, September 20, 1830, M234 R315.

6. Ibid.

7. Henry Rowe Schoolcraft, *Personal Memoirs of a Residence of Thirty Years with the Indian Tribes on the American Frontiers: With Brief Notices of Passing Events, Facts, and Opinions, A.D. 1812 to A.D. 1842* (Philadelphia: Lippincott, Grambo, 1851), 274; Bremer, *Indian Agent*, 105.

8. Scanlan, "Nicolas Boilvin," 149–150; Peter L. Scanlan, *Prairie du Chien: French, British, American* (Prairie du Chien, WI: Prairie du Chien Historical Society, 1998), 196–197.

9. "St. Peter's Indian Agency Handbook," unpublished manuscript on file at the Minnesota Historical Society, 21–26.

10. Juliette Kinzie, *Wau-Bun: The "Early Day" in the North-West* (Urbana: University of Illinois Press, 1992), 61.

11. Louise P. Kellogg, "The Agency House at Fort Winnebago," *Wisconsin Magazine of History* 14, no. 4 (June 1931): 438.

12. Kinzie, *Wau-Bun*, 1992 edition, 43.

13. Kinzie, *Wau-Bun*, 1992 edition, 181.

14. Kellogg, "The Agency House," 438; Kinzie, *Wau-Bun*, 265–266; Kinzie to Cass, October 15, 1830, M1 R27.

15. Amy Rosebrough, staff archaeologist, Wisconsin Historical Society, to Destinee Udelhoven, Old Indian Agency House director, December 3, 2009. On file at the Old Indian Agency House Museum, Portage, Wisconsin.

16. Kinzie, *Wau-Bun*, 1992 edition, 196.

17. Kinzie, *Wau-Bun*, 1992 edition, 196.

18. Kinzie, *Wau-Bun*, 1992 edition, 47. It is believed the chief was buried in the hill just behind the agency house.

19. Kinzie to Porter, October 1, 1832, M1 R31.

20. Charlotte Ouisconsin Van Cleve, *"Three Score Years and Ten," Life-Long Memories of Fort Snelling, Minnesota, and Other Parts of the West* (Minneapolis: Printing House of Harrison & Smith, 1888), 98.

Chapter 10

1. "An Act to Provide the Means of Extending the Benefits of Vaccination," May 5, 1832, *US Public Statues at Large*, vol. 4 (Boston: Charles C. Little and James Brown, 1846).

2. Diane Pearson, "Lewis Cass and the Politics of Disease: The Indian Vaccination Act of 1832," *Wicazo Sa Review* (2003): 10.

3. Ibid., 11.

4. An excellent examination of Andrew Jackson's Indian policy and the rationale behind it can be found in Ronald N. Satz, *American Indian Policy in the Jacksonian Era* (Lincoln: University of Nebraska Press, 1974).

5. Pearson, "Lewis Cass and the Politics of Disease," 10.

6. "Narrative of Andrew J. Vieau, Sr.," *Collections of the State Historical Society of Wisconsin*, vol. 11 (Madison: State Historical Society of Wisconsin, 1895), 225.

7. John Kinzie to Lewis Cass, August 27, 1832, M234 R931.

8. Juliette Kinzie, *Wau-Bun: The "Early Day" in the North-West* (Urbana: University of Illinois Press, 1992), 215.

9. Elbert Herring to William Clark, June 27, 1833 Senate Doc. 512, vol. 3, 724–725; "Treaty with the Chippewa, etc., 1833," found in *Charles J. Indian Affairs Laws and Treaties. vol. 2* (Treaties 1778–1883) (Washington: Government Printing Office, 1904), 402–415.

10. Marlin Garner and Benjamin H. Aylworth, *The Domestic Physician and Family Assistant: In Four Parts* (Cooperstown, NY: H. and E. Phinney, 1836), Applewood Books edition (Bedford, MA: Applewood Books, 2002), 103–105.

11. "Narrative of Spoon Decorah," *Collections of the State Historical Society of Wisconsin*, vol. 13 (Madison: State Historical Society of Wisconsin, 1895), 452.

12. Harstad, Peter T. "Disease and Sickness on the Wisconsin Frontier: Smallpox and Other Diseases," *Wisconsin Magazine of History* 43, no. 4 (Spring 1960): 255.

13. Kinzie to Porter, August 27, 1832, M1 R31; John W. Hall, *Uncommon Defense: Indian Allies in the Black Hawk War* (Cambridge, MA: Harvard University Press, 2009), 208–210.

14. Scott to Cass, August 19–21, 1832, in Ellen M. Whitney, ed., *The Black Hawk War, 1831–1832*, 2 vols. Collections of the Illinois Historical Library, vols. 35–38 (Springfield: Illinois Historical Library, 1970–78), vol. 2, 1024–1025; "Minutes of Examination of Prisoners, August 19, 1832," in Whitney, *Black Hawk War*, vol. 2, 1028–1033.

15. Kinzie to Porter, August 27, 1832, M1 R31.

16. Hall, *Uncommon Defense,* 211–212.

17. Ibid.; Treaty with the Winnebago, 1832, September 15, 1832, 7 Stat., 370, Proclamation, February 13, 1833, http://digital.library.okstate.edu/kappler/Vol2/treaties/win0345.htm.

18. Elbert Herring to Joseph Street, March 5, 1833, Senate doc. 512, vol. 3, 606; Elbert Herring to William Clark, June 27, 1833, Senate doc. 512, vol. 3, 725.

19. Herring to Street, March 5, 1833 Senate doc. 512, vol. 3, 192–193.

20. Kinzie, *Wau-Bun*, 1992 edition, 258; John Kinzie to George B. Porter, March 27, 1833, Senate doc. 512, vol. 4, 606.

21. Kinzie, *Wau-Bun*, 1992 edition, 247–248.

22. Ibid., 260.

23. Kinzie to Porter, March 27, 1833, US Bureau of Indian Affairs Copied Documents, 1616–1906, Wisconsin Historical Society Archives, hereafter referred to as WHS US BIA Copied Docs.

24. Herring to Porter, March 30, 1833 Senate doc. 512, vol. 3, 636.

25. Henry Dodge to Lewis Cass, May 3, 1833 Senate doc. 512, vol. 4, 202.

26. Kinzie to Porter, October 1, 1832, M1 R31.

27. Clarence E. Carter, ed., *The Territorial Papers of the United States, vol. 12: The Territory of Michigan, 1829–1837* (Washington, DC: United States Government Printing Office, 1945), 581–582.

28. Herring to Porter, March 2, 1833, WHS US BIA Copied Docs.

29. Kinzie, *Wau-Bun*, 1992 edition, 255.

30. Louise P. Kellogg, "The Agency House at Fort Winnebago," *Wisconsin Magazine of History* 14, no. 4 (June 1931): 446–447.

31. Samuel Stambaugh to General Atkinson, August 13, 1832, in Whitney, *Black Hawk War*, 995; Henry Dodge to John Kinzie, January 5, 1833, and John Kinzie to George Porter, March 15, 1832, both in WHS US BIA Copied Docs; Hall, *Uncommon Defense*, 219, 331.

32. Kinzie to Porter, March 15, 1833, WHS US BIA Copied Docs.

33. Kinzie, *Wau-Bun*, 1992 edition, 261.

34. Kinzie, *Wau-Bun*, 1992 edition, 262.

35. Porter to McCabe, September 23, 1833, in Joseph Greusel, ed., *Historical Collections: Collections and Researches Made by the Pioneer and Historical Soc. of the State of Michigan*, vol. 37 (Lansing, MI: Wyankoop, Hallenbeck, Crawford Co., 1909–1910), 285–286.

36. Mason to Cutler, August 23, 1834, in Greusel, *Michigan Historical Collections*, vol. 37, 297; Herring to Cutler, July 22, 1834, in Carter, ed., *Territorial Papers*, vol. 12, 789.

Chapter 11

1. For an overview of Potawatomi troubles after 1827, see R. David Edmunds, *The Potawatomis, Keepers of the Fire* (Norman: University of Oklahoma Press, 1978), 230–248. An assessment of the link between the Uprising of 1827 and the Chicago Treaty of 1833 can be found in William Franz, "Troubled with Them No More: The Winnebago War and Its Role as a Catalyst to

Indian Removal and the Chicago Treaty of 1833" (master's thesis, Northeastern Illinois University, 2003).

2. John D. Hager, "The American Fur Company and the Chicago of 1812–1835," *Journal of the Illinois State Historical Society (1908–1984)* 61, no. 2 (Summer 1968): 135–136; "Treaty with the Chippewa, etc., 1833," September 26, 1833, 7 Stat., 431, Proclamation, February 21, 1835, http://digital .library.okstate.edu/kappler/Vol2/treaties/chi0402.htm.

3. Milo M. Quaife, "The Chicago Treaty of 1833," *Wisconsin Magazine of History* 1, no. 3 (March 1918): 290; Anselm J. Gerwing, "The Chicago Treaty of 1833," *Journal of the Illinois State Historical Society (1908–1984)*, 57, no. 2 (Summer 1964): 135–136.

4. Louise P. Kellogg, "The Removal of the Winnebago," *Transactions of the Wisconsin Academy of Sciences, Arts, and Letters* 21 (1924): 26–27; Satterlee Clark, "Early Times and Events at Fort Winnebago," *Collections of the State Historical Society of Wisconsin*, vol. 8 (Madison: State Historical Society of Wisconsin, 1895), 318.

5. Henry Merrell, "Pioneer Life in Wisconsin," *Report and Collections of the State Historical Society of Wisconsin*, vol. 7 (Madison: State Historical Society of Wisconsin, 1895), 139, 141.

6. Merrell, "Pioneer Life," 393; Mark Diedrich, *Ho-Chunk Chiefs: Winnebago Leadership in an Era of Crisis* (Rochester, MN: Coyote Books, 2001), 118.

7. Ibid., 393.

8. John Porter Bloom, ed., *The Territorial Papers of the United States, vol. 27: The Territory of Wisconsin, 1836–1839; Executive Journal, 1836–1848* (Washington, DC: National Archives and Records Service Government Services Administration, 1969), 1090–1091.

9. Yellow Thunder's original land patent is on file at the Sauk County Historical Society in Baraboo, Wisconsin. Blue Wing's land patent can be seen online at the US Department of Interior, Bureau of Land Management website, www.glorecords.blm.gov/, land patents, document no. 13808.

10. Lawrence W. Onsager, "The Removal of the Winnebago Indians from Wisconsin in 1873–74" (master's thesis, Loma Linda University, 1985), 60–63; "Recollections of Indian Days," *Baraboo Weekly News*, July 18, 1918; Erhart A. Mueller, *Only in Sumpter* (Stevens Point, WI: Worzalla, 1977), 11–13.

11. C. G. B. Goodspeed, "Life and Services of William H. Holden, 1843–1922," *Journal of the Illinois State Historical Society* 15, no. 3/4 (October 1922–January 1923): 704.

12. Robert Fergus, *Directory of the City of Chicago, 1839*, Fergus' Historical Series no. 2 (Chicago: Fergus Print. Co., 1876); Patrick E. McClear, "Speculation, Promotion, and the Panic of 1837 in Chicago," *Journal of the Illinois State Historical Society (1908–1984)* 62, no. 2 (Summer 1969): 139.

13. William Hudson Harper and Charles H. Ravell, *Fifty Years of Banking in Chicago* (Chicago: Merchants' Loan and Trust Company, 1907), 79–80.

14. Fergus, *Directory of the City of Chicago, 1839*.

15. Ibid., part 1, 28.

16. Letter to "H," July 9, 1834, Morris Sleight Papers, Chicago History Museum.

17. Harriet Martineau, "Chicago in 1836, Strange Early Days," Fergus' Historical Series no. 9, 39.

18. Ibid., 40.

19. "The Kinzie Family in America," Fergus' Historical Series no. 30, 49; Eleanor Kinzie Gordon to Jefferson Davis, September 1, 1864, Museum of the Confederacy; Jefferson Davis, "Indian Policy of the United States," *North American Review* 143, no. 360 (November 1886): 444; Francis B. Heitman, *Historical Register and Dictionary of the United States: 1789–1908* (Baltimore: Genealogical, 1994), 602–603.

20. "The Kinzie Family in America," 48.

21. "Dropsy of the chest" was the cause of death listed in a notice regarding Kinzie's death in the *Cleveland Daily Leader*, Monday, June 26, 1865.

22. Juliette Kinzie, "Sketch of the Late Col. John H. Kinzie," *Addresses Delivered at the Annual Meeting of the Chicago Historical Society, November 29, 1868*, Fergus' Historical Series, vol. 20, 1877, 26; notice of Kinzie's death was posted in the *Cleveland Daily Leader*, Cleveland, Ohio, Monday, June 26, 1865.

Chapter 12

1. Bertha A. Holbrook, "The Old Indian Agency House at Portage," *Wisconsin Magazine of History* 29, no. 1 (September 1945): 36.

2. Ibid., 37–41; Louise P. Kellogg, "The Agency House at Fort Winnebago," *Wisconsin Magazine of History* 14, no. 4 (June 1931): 437–449.

3. A chronicle of the renovation of the Indian Agency House can be seen on the museum's Facebook page, www.facebook.com/pages/Historic-Indian-Agency-House-at-Fort-Winnebago/103130967332.

4. Michelle M. Greendeer, "Purchasing Back 'Our Lands,'" *Hocak Worak* (Ho-Chunk Nation), November 12, 2003; John Kozlowicz, "Land Returned to HCN," *Hocak Worak* (Ho-Chunk Nation), May 23, 2001.

5. Richard W. Jaeger, "Once Again, Ho-Chunk Land Is the ISSUE," *Wisconsin State Journal*, April 23, 1996.

6. Elizabeth Brixey, "Tribe's Request Spurs Questions," *Wisconsin State Journal*, January 3, 1996.

7. "Comment to Proposed Rules Regarding 25 CFR Part 151 Acquisition of Title Land in Trust," Proceedings of the Sauk County Board of Supervisors, April 1999–March 2000, 224.

8. Scott DeLaurelle, "County Appeals Land Acquisition," *Baraboo News Republic*, March 21, 2005.

9. Tim Damos, "Ho-Chunk to Receive Ammo Plant Land," *Baraboo News Republic*, December 7, 2014; Kim Lamoreaux, "Let Her Heal," *Sauk Prairie Eagle*, June 26, 2015.

INDEX

Page numbers in *italics* refer to illustrations.

ABOUT THE AUTHOR

Peter Shrake is a lifelong resident of Wisconsin. He earned his master's degree from the University of Wisconsin–Eau Claire, focusing on Jacksonian Indian policy in Wisconsin. He also earned a master's degree of library and information studies from the University of Wisconsin.

Shrake served as the executive director of the Sauk County Historical Museum for eight years. For three years he worked as a reference archivist for the Wisconsin Historical Society Library and Archives. Since 2011, he has been the archivist at Circus World Museum. He lives in Baraboo with his wife, Kim, and his sons, Ethan and Ben.